Presented to

Margaret and Sam

by

Kialeen and Lee

Date

August 28, 1993

May this book set the pace and be a reminder to always put Jesus first in your personal lives and your marriage. May our Lord Jesus Christ (the anointed one) richly bless you as a couple.

Daily Devotions for Newlyweds

Davis Cooper

BROADMAN PRESS
Nashville, Tennessee

Dewey Decimal Classification: 242.2
Subject Heading: DEVOTIONS, DAILY
Library of Congress Catalog Card Number: 81-67204
Printed in the United States of America

About the Author

Davis L. Cooper is pastor of University Hills Baptist Church, Denver, Colorado, having previously served churches in Louisiana and Oklahoma as pastor. He holds degrees from Baylor University (B.A.) and Southwestern Baptist Theological Seminary (B.D.) and has done graduate study at Louisiana State University. Davis grew up in Argentina as the son of missionaries and is a third-generation preacher. He has been married to Jean Priddy since 1955; they are the parents of four grown children. Davis's hobbies are snow-skiing, golfing, and reading, especially theological works.

Preface

There are several reasons why I hope you have not overlooked this part of this book. One reason is that I want to introduce myself. We will be sharing in some very special moments, and I'd like for you to know something about me. I am a preacher who does a lot of premarital counseling. I have been married for more than twenty-six years to the most wonderful person I know. We have four children; and, in the process of these years, we have passed through many of the problems you will encounter in your journey. A lot of what I have written has come out of a life of reading which has been distilled through my own personal experiences.

Another reason I am glad you're reading this page is that I want to suggest some ways you might best use this book. The first is that it must be used with the Bible. Unless our devotional exercises keep us in the Word of God, they are useless. I hope you have your own personal quiet time with the Father. I hope you are implementing a plan to read through the Bible. If you are not, my prayer is that as a result of our time together you will love the Bible and love the time you spend studying it.

My next suggestion is that you plan a definite time to use this little book each day. The time you spend will not be long, but the regular daily discipline will be valuable personally and will help you learn some good lessons about marital communication. It doesn't matter what time you choose. Some folks like the early morning; others can't concentrate early in the day. Some couples like to close the day with devotional study and prayer; others fall asleep in front of the television during the news. You choose the time that is right for the two of you, and make sure it is a time together.

That leads to my next suggestion. You need to learn together the joy of sharing together about the love of the Father. If you are not going through this journey together, many of the ideas in this book aren't going to make much sense.

My next suggestion has to do with the things which I sometimes will ask you to do. At first they may seem artificial and strained. Try to do them anyway. If nothing else, you will learn how to do the most difficult thing in the world: talk *with* someone you love instead of talking *to* him or her. After you have done this for several weeks you won't need any encouragement from me. You will come to anticipate with excitement these moments of sharing.

My last suggestion is that you keep a hymn book handy and read or sing the hymns which you feel best fit what God is saying to you each day. Let these brief moments become worship which inspires and refreshes your day.

Each week you will discover a different devotional theme. Allow yourself to live in each theme each week. These are the concepts I have found to be so important in the most profound earthly relationship God created.

Finally, I am dedicating this book to my wife, Jean. She is the most beautiful and caring person I know. She has loved me into understanding many of the things I am sharing with you, and she is my best friend.

God bless you.

D. L. C.
Denver, Colorado
Summer 1981

Sun 8/29

Week 1, Day 1
IN THE BEGINNING
Read Genesis 1:1

In the beginning. This is a beginning, isn't it? A beginning in this book as it leads you into the Book. A beginning in your relationship, which has the promise to be the best thing that can happen to a man and a woman.

Wouldn't it be nice if some warranty would absolutely guarantee the success of your marriage? Of course, there's no such thing. But good beginnings strongly affect positive outcomes. Good planting, good harvest. Good foundations, solid buildings. Good start, good marriage. Beginnings are important.

That which begins ought also to live out its full life cycle. For example, you do not live cut off from either your past or your future. There are only two of you here, but think of what has gone on in the past and what is going to be. Today is vitally important because it is the realized promise of yesterday and the hope which will be fulfilled tomorrow. Yesterday, today, and tomorrow—all of that is part of the beginning of your marriage.

In the beginning . . . God. No way to begin right without him. To recognize *the fact* and to know *the person* are vital. Two important ideas spin out of this significant statement. The world you have been married in is a world made by God the Father. What an amazing perspective that lends to life! The other fascinating idea is the responsibility which is yours as you structure your marital relationship according to his will. It really isn't your world or your house or your time or your marriage. It is all his, and he has called us to share it all with him. *In the beginning . . . God!*

Take just a few minutes to share with each other your answers to these two questions:

1. What will you do with this gift of your wedding day to enhance and strengthen your relationship?

2. What are your plans and dreams for the future that will make good use of your lives up until now?

Pray that God will be with you in this, your beginning together—and every day.

Week 1, Day 2
MADE IN HIS IMAGE
Read Genesis 1:26-31

Have you ever made something which was so obviously the work of your hands that you did not have to identify it as being yours? Famous artisans build that quality into their works. A person who appreciates art can clearly distinguish the works of Michelangelo, da Vinci, Rubens, and Rembrandt. More recently, the western art of Remington and Russell is easily identified. Their distinctive personalities and craftsmanship have been transferred to canvas, wood, and marble. There is no need for a manufacturer's stamp to identify the maker.

So it is with the most beautiful work of creation which the world has ever known: the two of you! (and everyone else in the human race!) The Bible reminds us of something we too easily forget. We are the only part of all of creation which has the personal touch which identifies us as being God's work. We are made in his image!

It's not that we look like God. But he has made us able to have fellowship with him. And he has made us alone able to glory in his work and respond to his love. He has made us able to have dominion over the other things he created. He has made us to rule as stewards over all he has made. And he has made us so that, of all his creatures, we alone may choose to go against our nature and our Father.

Being made in his image has obvious implications about who is really boss. But more than that, what does it say about how we treat each other? Can masterpieces do less than honor each other?

Think about what this means in your new marriage. Hasn't God created something wonderful in your new spouse? Why not tell him or her so?

Take just a few minutes to say to each other: "You are God's masterpiece. Because you are his masterpiece, I promise. . . . " (You finish the statement in your own words.)

Pray, thanking God for his wonderful creation of the two of you, and asking him to help you to remember that fact always.

Tᴇ 8/31

Week 1, Day 3
MADE NOT TO BE ALONE
Read Genesis 2:18

Loneliness is probably the worst feeling a person can experience. You can be lonely anywhere—all by yourself or in the middle of a million people.

Being alone is something different, though. Being alone is a choice you make for specific times. You may choose to be alone for the sake of privacy, for the sake of hurt and healing, or to be in fellowship with our Father in prayer.

But being alone is not forever. We can also choose not to be alone. Not being alone is what you were made for. God said, "It is not good for the man to be alone. I will make a helper suitable for him." Loneliness comes with all its hurt when you do not experience the reason and purpose of our creation. You are made to reach, not simply to fold your arms. You are made to give and to take.

You are made for fellowship with God. To experience that in all its fullness is essential to being not lonely. Only he can satisfy the thirst and hunger for him. But he has also made us for each other. As parts of a jigsaw puzzle, we are made to fit with each other.

Imagine being without your mate—not having the warmth of his or her voice, the comfort of his or her arms. Still, you need time alone with God to renew and refresh yourselves. Then you can come back to enrich your marriage.

Take a few minutes to answer these questions for each other:

1. Do I sometimes abuse your aloneness as I try to overcome my loneliness?

2. Do I sometimes push you into loneliness because I insist on my aloneness?

3. Do we seek to fit ourselves together like puzzle pieces so that the complete picture can bring the joy God wants us to have?

Pray, thanking God for making you for himself and each other, and asking his forgiveness for the times you deny him and each other the fellowship only you can give.

WED 9/1

Week 1, Day 4
THE FIRST WEDDING CEREMONY
Read Genesis 2:21-22

Remember all the times you fell in and out of love as you were growing up? Heights of ecstacy! Pits of despair! Then you found each other. You got to know each other. You became good friends and decided you really couldn't live without each other.

You planned your wedding. What chaos! What madness! At times you wondered what you had gotten yourself into.

Then you heard the music that signaled the moment. You were either standing between the preacher and your best man or you were walking down the aisle, hanging on to your daddy's arm.

Remember how it was and what you felt? Is that the guy who thought a tank top was a dress shirt? Is she the girl whose wardrobe consisted only of ragged blue jeans? Who is that stranger in that tuxedo? Who is that vision in white?

In that first wedding so long ago, God walked the new bride down the aisle. And fathers have been imitating the Father ever since. And men have felt like they were waking up from a nap to see a dream coming toward them. And women have felt like they were the star of the show!

But nothing really happens until the promises are made. Vows and promises in love and marriage are like heavy wire and electricity. They serve to direct and focus power. Without these promises our powerful feelings remain unverbalized and uncommitted. We commit ourselves to a great task in a great context.

What did you promise each other? What commitments did you make?

Take a few minutes to repeat your vows to each other. If you don't remember them, repeat these. "I promise to listen to you with my heart as well as my ears. I promise to respect you without making you earn my respect. I promise to be faithful to you in every way. I promise to forgive you when you fail to live up to these promises. I promise this because I love you and I want our love to grow into all that God wants it to be."

Pray, thanking God for bringing you together, and asking him to remember always your promises of love and faithfulness.

Week 1, Day 5
JUST WHAT I NEEDED!
Read Genesis 2:23

Being the new kid on the block is not a pleasant feeling. This was Adam's problem. He was the last touch of God's creative order, and he was different. Boy, was he different from everything else! Adam was the first one to find out that *three's a crowd*. Two plants and Adam. Two dogs and Adam. Two dinosaurs and Adam! Something definitely was missing!

Adam had God, of course. But even God knew that Adam needed somebody just like himself. Remember that God made Adam in his image, and part of that means fellowship. By definition, fellowship means at least two who have something significant in common.

God and Adam may have looked around for a while. But there was nothing Adamlike in the whole place. So the Lord anesthetized Adam. He performed surgery, and God made a somebody with the part of Adam that was closest to his heart.

You can imagine Adam's reaction when he awoke to see this beautiful work of God standing before him. "Hot Dog!" may be the closest we could get to the spirit of the words recorded in Genesis. "Just like me. Just what I needed."

Perhaps you're feeling the same way about your new mate. That's great! God can richly bless the two of you as he blessed Adam with Eve. All you have to do is let him guide your marriage.

Take a few minutes to answer these questions for each other:

1. Can you imagine what life would be like if there were nobody for you?

2. Do you express your need for your spouse to him or her, or do you only use him or her?

Pray, thanking God for this special person just like you in your life, and asking him to help you remember that a gift is best received when it is honored as the giver wishes.

Week 1, Day 6
THE REASON FOR IT ALL!
Read Genesis 2:24

Why did you get married? Don't give me all the mushy stuff. Just tell me the cold, rational reasons.

What a laugh! Whoever gets married for cold, rational reasons? Nevertheless, think about these reasons for a moment.

Well, you had this strange and wonderful and agonizing feeling for each other. You couldn't stay apart. Your friends got sick looks on their faces when they were around you. The Greeks called it *eros,* the most powerful of all human emotions. It makes people do terrible and marvelous things—like getting married! So you did.

Then there was the fact that, for as long as you could remember, people you know have been getting married. It was the expected thing for folks to do at a certain age. You grow up and you get married. So you did.

Then there were your mom and dad. They put a lot of stock in marriage. They were married themselves, and they seemed to recommend it highly. In fact, they were always particular about the people you felt really close to. When you told them you were getting married, they were as pleased as if they'd made the choice for you. So you got married.

Is that the real reason, the only reason? The Bible says, "For this reason." That means there is a bigger reason than any you've thought up. The reason people get married is because the Lord plans it that way. Without even realizing it, they are doing it to please him. We act out his plans sometimes without even knowing or caring that they are his plans. But when we do know and we do care, then we keep him in our hearts and his plans in our minds. Marriage for the right reason is the source of great happiness and satisfaction.

Take a few minutes to answer this question to each other: Did we get married for God's reason?

Pray, thanking God for this plan of marriage, and asking him to help you remember to consult him before making plans for your new family.

Week 1, Day 7
NAKED BUT NOT ASHAMED
Read Genesis 2:25

Confidence is essential to a lack of fear. Lack of fear is essential to the absence of self-consciousness. The absence of self-consciousness is essential to being unashamed. That's a lot of essentials, isn't it? But think about it for a moment when you imagine Adam and Eve walking around unclothed and unaware of it.

They were confident that they were exactly where they were supposed to be. The Father had put them there, hadn't he? They had no fear because they knew nothing about hurt or harm. They were not self-conscious or ashamed because they didn't know any other way to feel.

They became aware of themselves, and they hid from each other and God. Modesty in dress and attitude has been the result ever since. That's the way it ought to be. Proper modesty is a sign of respect for others and a request for respect.

Modern standards seem to oppose traditional modesty. But we are most modest with those we care for the most. It would be unrealistic and naive for us to pretend that we could recapture the innocence of the Garden of Eden.

Yet there are special times when marriage partners are ready to be open in all ways with each other. In those times our fears recede, our self-consciousness fades, our confidence returns, and we can be unashamed and modest and naked. Those moments are gifts from God.

Take a few minutes to answer this question for each other: What would happen eventually if your partner forced you into a false expression of openness?

Pray, asking God to teach you that modesty and openness are not contradictory when you both deeply love him and each other.

Week 2, Day 1
PRAISE HIM! PRAISE HIM!
Read Psalm 103:1-2

How important is it that the people around you maintain positive attitudes? The person with a genuine positive attitude usually helps you to be glad that another day has dawned. Nothing helps a developing relationship more than positive attitudes.

When it comes to positive thinking, nothing beats the Bible. The key to a positive outlook in the Bible is the consistent praise of God. Praise can become mechanical when our lips are disconnected from our hearts and sometimes from our minds. Praise which starts in our hearts, refreshes our minds, and streams from our lips will transform darkness into daylight!

Praise does two things: It gets our minds off of ourselves and the circumstances which temporarily darken our perspective. It also focuses our attention upon the one whose love never fails. Praise is the channel of transcendence. Someone outside of us and beyond us wishes to move into our lives with power and joy, but he has no way to come in until praise builds a highway.

Most of us do not begin praising the Father until we feel like it; and we don't feel like it until we are aware of something worth praising. We often conveniently forget about the multitude of things worth praising him for. Does that strike a tender spot? The psalmist recognized that tendency in his own life. So he kept on reminding himself not to forget all of God's benefits.

Take a few minutes to share with your partner at least three things for which you are thankful.

Pray, praising God for the gifts of your lives, including your marriage.

Week 2, Day 2
DOCTOR GOD
Read Psalm 103:3

When I was growing up, our pastor was also our family doctor. He was a saintly, compassionate man. I grew up thinking all doctors were like him. Of course, they are not. With mature reflection, I suspect he was not as perfect as I thought.

Perhaps it is natural to think of doctors in a special way. We rarely have any contact with them until we are hurting. They become our means of healing. They seem to do what we cannot do for ourselves; so we put them in a special category. Then sometimes we become hostile when they slip off the pedestal we've put them on.

The truth is that doctors can never be more than what we are—human beings. In fact, doctors don't even heal us. We heal us. They help the process through their medical knowledge. Doctors are not gods. We only make ourselves and them miserable when we pretend they are.

What happens when you place your marriage partner on that kind of pedestal? Just like doctors, your partner is only human. He or she will fail you many times in your marriage. So don't expect more than he or she can provide.

However, God is the true doctor. He heals all your diseases. He does not always meet your expectations, but he is your healer. He does it in all kinds of ways—from providing you the comfort of your partner's touch to healing your hurts in times of loneliness. All real healing originates in him.

Take a few minutes to share these things with your partner:

1. A time when one of your parents showed his or her humanness by failing you.

2. A time when God worked through another person to heal a personal hurt.

Pray, thanking God for healing your hurts, and asking him to help each of you to accept the other's humanness.

Tue 9/7

Week 2, Day 3
HE LIFTED ME OUT OF THE MIRY CLAY
Read Psalm 103:4

Doubt has troubled people ever since just before man was ushered out of the Garden of Eden. The beginning of an awful lot of frustration and misery was when doubt snaked its way into the hearts of the first parents.

After only a little over a week of marriage, you likely have not had any doubts about married life. The time will come, though, when you will wonder what you are doing married to this man or this woman. Such doubt is only human, though.

There is a major temptation for doubt by the two of you as a couple. That is to doubt the importance of your new involvement as a married couple in church. When the normal doubts of life occur, both of you need the spiritual resource of the church.

Where do doubts originate? One source of doubt is our forgetfulness about what our lives were like and would still be like if God had not done what he did for us. Imagine your misery if God had not allowed the two of you to marry.

The psalmist puts it forcefully: "He redeems my life from the pit." That is the act of rescue on God's part. He takes care of the negative realities of your experience. But he doesn't leave you there. "He crowns me with love and compassion." What a contrast! Out of hell into heaven. From death unto life. Out of the pit and on the throne. And the crown I wear is his steadfast love and tender mercy.

Take a few minutes to share with your partner a time when you doubted him or her and how God led you from that doubt.

Pray, asking God to forgive you for the times you have doubted each other and him and to help you to keep him involved in your marriage.

Week 2, Day 4
THE REAL GUSTO OF LIFE
Read Psalm 103:5

Cotton candy. Memories flood my mind when I think of cotton candy. And sicken my stomach! I still recall the feeling that nothing ever tasted quite as good on first bite. The other memory is my stomach arguing back as I left the dusty little county fair.

There are two lessons which cotton candy lovers invariably learn: One, you can't make a regular meal out of it. Two, by the time you think you've had enough, you've had too much! In other words, cotton candy won't satisfy you, just like many other things you think are going to provide real satisfaction.

A television commercial used to urge you to grab all the gusto you could because you only go around once in life. That's true. Everybody only goes around once in life. There are no seconds or overs. So you must take advantage of each opportunity that comes knocking.

But another truth is that nobody can grab gusto. It always comes in the side door while you are doing something else.

Can the two of you experience gusto—or real satisfaction—in your marriage? The answer is a resounding YES! But real satisfaction in marriage comes as a by-product of following Christ as the head of your home. In fact, the psalmist puts it this way: "He satisfies my mouth with good things so that my youth is renewed like the eagle's."

Take a few minutes to review with each other the ways you've been reaching for gusto. Answer this question for each other: Can we have real satisfaction in our marriage without Christ as our Lord?

Pray, thanking God for the joys of life, and asking him to lead you to experience real satisfaction in your marriage.

Week 2, Day 5
THE OTHER SHOE
Read Psalm 103:8-9

A man with huge bags under his eyes, hands shaking, barely able to speak, went to a psychiatrist. His anxiety was caused by the strange habits of a person who had recently moved into the room just above. One night when the man was almost asleep, the new tenant above dropped a heavy shoe on the floor. Jarred awake by the sound, the man had decided to wait until the other shoe was dropped before trying to sleep. He waited and waited; nothing happened. The same thing happened night after night. His anxiety finally became unbearable. Eventually the man discovered that the new tenant had only one leg—thus, only one shoe to take off!

Do you recall how much time in your life you have spent waiting for the other shoe to drop? This is especially true in relationships. Take, for instance, the times you did something your parents told you not to do. You waited, dreading what they would do to you when they found out.

The interesting thing about this kind of thinking is that many of us have the same feelings about God. Some of us have the idea that his scepter is really a fly swatter, and he's just waiting for us to get comfortable so he can swat us.

Contrary to this kind of thinking, the psalmist saw a different quality in the Father: "The Lord is compassionate and gracious, slow to anger, abounding in love. He will not always accuse, nor will he harbor his anger forever." We have no reason to wait for the other shoe to drop.

God wants newlyweds to avoid the _other-shoe syndrome_. He wants you to follow his example.

Take a few minutes to share with each other one of your _other-shoe_ experiences. Then discuss how you can follow God's example to avoid similar incidents in your marriage.

Pray, asking God to forgive you for forgetting that he is compassionate and slow to anger, and asking him to help the two of you to be patient and understanding.

Week 2, Day 6
THE GREAT DISAPPEARING ACT
Read Psalm 103:10-12

I've got a confession. I don't believe in magic. But I am fascinated by magicians. Where does all that stuff go that they make disappear? I know it is somewhere, but where? I know it's all a trick. But it still fascinates me.

Have you ever wished you could make things disappear? I can remember quite a few things: report cards, incriminating evidence, myself when I make dumb remarks! Take a few moments right now to make your own mental list of things you'd like to disappear.

Now that you've made the list, close your eyes and wish them all away: all the bills, all the pounds, all the ugly memories. They are all gone, right? Wrong! The truth is we can only do what magicians do: shift junk around.

That is what is so frustrating about sin: There is no way to get around sin. When you sin, you can't get rid of it. You can make resolutions. You can turn over new leaves. You can shuffle the junk around. But there it still sits, grinning devilishly at you.

No human being can ever get rid of sin. But God can and does. "As far as the east is from the west, so far has he removed our transgressions from us." Do you know how far east is from west? Now that is a disappearing act!

First John 1:9 promises, "If we confess our sins, he is faithful and just to forgive us our sins and to cleanse us from all unrighteousness." The same should be true in marriage. We should be able to confess our sins to one another as well as to God.

Take a few minutes to answer these questions for each other: Do I feel free to confess my mistakes to you? Will you forgive me when I fail you?

Pray, asking God to help you feel the freedom to confess your sins to him and to each other.

Week 2, Day 7
JUST LIKE A LOVING DADDY!
Read Psalm 103:13

Some people have memories of their parents which are not very pleasant. In fact, the words *mother* and *father* have been ruined for these people. That's very sad. All I need to do to brighten my day is to bring the faces of my two wonderful parents to mind. If I think about them very long I start laughing; then I cry. I'm not sad; they have simply been the source of much happiness in my life.

That's the way everybody should be able to think about their parents. Why is this so important? When the Bible describes what God is like, it says repeatedly that God is a father like our fathers.

You may be one of those who thinks, if God is a father like my father, I'd just as soon forget him. If you are, look at it this way: God is the father your father should have been. God is a perfect Father. His love is without limits, and his discipline is administered in tenderness and patience.

Jesus said to call him "Abba." That's the word a little Jewish boy would use when he climbed into his father's lap to tell him all the wonderful things which had happened. It means *daddy*. There is no other word which captures more tenderly that special relationship. We may address him as *Almighty God* or *Eternal, Heavenly Father,* but he wants us to feel as close to him as a little child feels toward his daddy.

Take a few minutes to share with each other some of the fun times with your parents that you remember. Then talk about how you feel about God as your Heavenly Father.

Pray, thanking God for each of your parents, and praising him for being your Heavenly Father.

Week 3, Day 1
WHO NEEDS TO PRAY?
Read Luke 11:1

Do you have trouble with prayer? Some people do, you know. Some feel silly telling God something he already knows. Some may wonder: who really needs to pray?

The Bible is filled with true stories of people who spent a lot of time praying. The one who intrigues me, however, is the one person who would not need to pray. That person is the Lord Jesus Christ. He was so obviously a man of prayer that his disciples asked him to teach them how to pray.

The prayer life of Jesus was not just a voluntary activity to provide a proper model for his followers. He needed to pray in order to remain in unbreakable fellowship with his Father.

Now, if Jesus needed to pray, what does that say about you and me? If I don't pray, I do not have conscious contact with the source of my being. If I don't pray, I don't have a chance to confess my sins. If I don't pray . . . the list goes on and on.

Take time today to think about prayer and why you need prayer. Take time to pray for each other.

As you sit at the table or side by side on the couch, talk to each other about what you believe prayer does. This may be difficult to do at first, but keep on trying. You will find that praying together in this way builds a bond in your home which will help you to stand the stresses of life.

Pray, asking God to teach you that you need to pray more than you want to pray.

Week 3, Day 2
TEACH US TO PRAY
Read Luke 11:1

Two things seem to be sure about people and learning nowadays: They want to learn a lot, and they want to learn it now! I have seen my children demonstrate these truths time and again. They have wanted to become instant athletes or instant cooks or instant scholars.

Where did we ever get the idea that instant is possible? Even instant foods have to be carefully prepared before we can do any of our instant magic with them!

Christians should not be surprised to discover that they need to learn how to pray. Somehow, many of us believe that prayer should be intuitive, like breathing. That's partly true. Our desire to pray is intuitive. It is our response to the magnetic pull of the Father. Thus, we don't need to learn to pray; we need to learn *how* to pray.

I believe that learning how to pray is much like learning a new language. Languages are learned. We even learn our native language, but most of us learn it poorly.

Prayer is not only a language; it is an art—the art of conversation. That art has to be learned, too, because most of us never get over filling empty seconds by praying with reference to ourselves. Monologues take less training than authentic dialogues.

Prayer is also an expression of fellowship. Being able to relate effectively to the Father is also something we must learn. We must pray to someone we do not see and do not hear. That is the toughest thing to learn. Yet the folks who learn to talk the Father's language find a fellowship with him that only they know.

Share with each other your first memories of prayer in your homes.

Pray, asking God to teach you how to pray so that you may receive what he wants to give.

Week 3, Day 3
LEARNING TO TALK WITH GOD
Read Luke 11:2

Have you ever made any unbelievably awful mistakes in your language? Norm Crosby, the deaf comic, makes a lot of money making mistakes. He plans it that way. Everybody knows he is pretending, and everyone has a good laugh.

Unfortunately, many of our attempts with languages are not so easily laughed off. I grew up in Argentina as a son of Southern Baptist missionaries. One day my mother came in from the market nearly hysterical. She had overheard a woman from England trying to purchase a chicken. Using her limited Portuguese (the language of Argentina), she had asked for the mother of an egg.

Talking with God is something which a person must learn. Even after we learn that we should pray, we must learn to *whom* we are talking and *how* we ought to talk.

The Bible teaches that God is high and lifted up. His ways are not our ways, and his thoughts are not our thoughts. We cannot crash the party when we come to talk with him. In fact, if we did not come through our mediator, Jesus Christ, we would have no right at all to speak with the Father. Perhaps realizing that the Father is high and lifted up helps us get into the proper attitude for prayer.

How do you approach God in prayer? Do you come reverently, conscious that it is only in Jesus Christ that you have access to the heavenly throne room?

Share your own experiences of prayer with each other—from your earliest memories until now. How much has your prayer life changed? How much greater do you want it to be?

Pray, thanking God that he is patiently willing to teach you how to talk to him.

Week 3, Day 4
FIRST THINGS FIRST
Read Luke 11:2

George W. Truett was the pastor of First Baptist Church, Dallas, Texas, from 1897 until 1944. He was considered by many to be the greatest preacher of his time.

Once my father-in-law shared with me that he had heard Dr. Truett preach several times. I was shocked when he told me that he had not been greatly impressed by Truett's preaching. But he quickly added that he had never heard anyone pray like George Truett. He said, "It was just like he was talking to his daddy."

How does a person learn to pray that way? We learn it when we are ready to put first things first. In simple language, we have learned how when we acknowledge God as supreme in our lives and when we make what he wants more important than what we want.

This truth is so obvious that we tend to bypass it. So let's back up a little and look closely at three expressions.

Father is the first. *Father* both in the closeness of relationship and caring and Father in total authority. You really can't say "Father" if you are not ready to submit to his authority. Do you say "Father" as if it all depended on him?

Hallowed is the next expression. It means holy, and it has reference to his name, which in turn refers to him. He is *holy*. His name is holy. Do you treat his name as holy?

Kingdom is the third expression. It means his total rule in every aspect of our lives. Does he rule every aspect of your marriage?

Take time to decide together upon one aspect of your new relationship that you have discovered to be crucial to your marriage. Agree together to give that aspect to God's power to redeem. Join hands and pray together.

Pray, asking God to help the two of you to treat his name as holy and to open every part of your marriage to his rule.

Week 3, Day 5
HE CARES ABOUT MY BREAD
Read Luke 11:3

Have you ever played the psychological game of "I never—You never"? You may not recognize it by that name, but it is a favorite played by adolescents of various ages. Some are teenagers, some are young adults, and some are older adults acting out of self-pity like adolescents.

The game is played most effectively when you don't think of it as a game. You begin with "I never" or "you never" and finish it with whatever comes to mind: for example, "I never do anything I want" or "you never let me do what other kids get to do." When you examine such dialogue, it sounds juvenile and petty, but it is a game all ages play sometimes.

The strangest form of this game is the one which is played in prayer. Remember that we reside in the midst of an abundance which is totally free. (Have you priced sunsets lately?) Sometimes our praying is contaminated with an attitude that seems to say: "I never get the things I ask for. You never hear anything I say. I never get to do things my way. You never bless me in the ways you do other people." Our recriminations can go on and on. The only surprise is that, when our list begins, we don't hear a heavenly window being slammed shut! But the Father is long-suffering and patient. Besides, he has heard all this from people more spiritual than us.

The fact is that the Father cares so much about what happens to us daily that he teaches us to pray, asking for the most mundane things.

Daily bread. What could be more ordinary than that? Do you suppose that he wants us to learn that everything, even daily needs, depend on him, and that learning to ask and say *thank you* about daily needs is one of the first steps to a true understanding of life—including marriage?

Recall for each other five needs for which God has provided. Write down and share five needs you will have today/tomorrow.

Pray, thanking God for his gracious provision and asking him to meet your specific needs today/tomorrow.

Week 3, Day 6
HELP FOR THE HARD SPOTS
Read Luke 11:4

Do you know how to protect yourself against dragons? Sound silly? Well, as a child I used to worry about such things. I usually called the resident knights, my parents. But they would usually say, "Count sheep, two at a time, and check with me in the morning." Why would you need them in the morning? Dragons can't be touched by the sunlight. (When I was small I often confused dragons and Dracula.) The method which finally saw me safely into adult life was to cover every inch of my body with a blanket. No dragons got me, but I nearly died of heat stroke several summer nights!

In prayer two *dragons* constantly undermine our efforts to grow up spiritually. One is *asking for forgiveness,* and the other is *avoiding temptation.* The problem with asking for forgiveness is that my asking is always tied to my willingness to forgive. I am not, by nature, forgiving. The problem with temptation is that while half of me is talking honestly with the Father, the other half of me is looking around to see what I can get into. What a mess! So what do you do about these dragons?

The truth is that both of these are beyond us anyway. Since it is beyond my nature to forgive and it is precisely my nature to yield to temptation, my only hope is for supernatural help. Forgiveness comes naturally to the Father. So I ask him to help me to forgive *in Christ.* That is very important. I am not asking that he make my nature strong enough to forgive, but that *Christ forgive through me.* If I do it in my strength, it becomes a source of pride, and I'm right back where I started. If he does it in Christ through me, then all I can do is stand back and watch miracles.

The same principle is true in the trials and temptations of marriage. Let him deal with your temptation and trust him to be adequate for every trial.

Share with each other the problems you have with forgiveness. Share how each can help the other with forgiving.

Pray, thanking the Father that he continues to forgive you while you are still learning to forgive.

Week 3, Day 7
KEEP ON KNOCKING!
Read Luke 11:5-13

Do you know any two-legged pests? You know, the kind who invariably show up at the wrong time and the wrong place and do not know the meaning of the word *no*. The mental image of such a person is enough to make most of us take solemn oaths never to become such.

Perhaps this is the reason most of us are not *pesty* in our prayers. We make one or two polite requests and, if nothing happens, like nice people we drop the whole matter.

I don't know if God wants us to nag or become pests, but one thing seems to be sure: He is not happy with our tendency to ask once and then clam up!

In the midst of the humor of this parable is this lesson: Don't quit knocking! Those who keep on knocking, keep on asking, keep on seeking will receive all that the Father wants to give them.

Why does the Father do things this way? Perhaps he is tired of our tendency to run in, ask, and run out. Maybe he wants us to sit down and talk to him about the whole thing. "Why do you need this thing?" "What are you going to do with it when you get it?" Those are just the kind of talks fathers like to have.

One thing is sure: God wants to give us more than we ever dream of asking for. He is a Father who is absolutely dependable in the quality of his gifts. If we ask for a fish, he will not bring a stone. If we pray for an egg, he will not send a scorpion. He wants to give us everything. But he wants us to keep on asking, keep on knocking, keep on seeking.

Take time to evaluate and share your personal prayer lives. Do you like to talk with the Father? Do you enjoy telling him about what is going on? Or are you afraid that, if you spend too much time, he might ask some embarrassing questions about why you want certain things? How easy is it for you to be honest with God?

Pray, asking God to teach you how to keep praying when answers don't come right away.

Week 4, Day 1
MOVING MOUNTAINS
Read Matthew 21:21

Now, about mountains. You can go over them, under them, through them, around them (on either side), or none of the above. *Or* you can move them. Of all the sayings of Jesus, this one may have caused more head scratching than all the rest put together.

The truth is: Nobody I know and nobody you know and nobody the disciples knew had ever seen anybody move a mountain. Nowadays it would take so long to get the appropriate permits and the environmental impact studies that you would be out of the mood of mountain moving anyway by the time permission was given.

Perhaps Jesus was not talking about just mountains. Maybe he was using them as an example for this point: God can do the impossible—the really impossible. He was not saying simply that God can do hard jobs. God can and will do whatever anybody considers to be impossible. The proof is found in the resurrection of Christ! Nothing could seem to be any more impossible than to give someone bodily life to never die again. God did that. God can also move mountains without even consulting our local bureaucrats.

The next step sounds almost like a copout. We can do the impossible if we have faith. That rules us all out, right? Wrong! Jesus didn't say we have to have enormous faith, only faith like a mustard seed. He doesn't say that we have to be free of doubts about everything, only that we should not waver in our request.

Remember, too, that faith and prayer are partners in these impossible enterprises.

Take time to share together some areas of your lives or marriage which you have always thought were too big for God. Talk together about asking and believing that God can and wants to do the impossible for you. Remember, his time schedule may not quite coincide with yours; so wait and keep on asking and believing.

Pray, asking God to forgive you for pulling him down to your size, and for helping you to have faith about impossible things.

Week 4, Day 2
THE PROOF OF THE PUDDING
Read Hebrews 11:1

When we all were children, we played wishing games. "Starlight, star bright, first star I see tonight. I wish I may, I wish I might, have the wish I wish tonight." Or you blew out all the candles on the birthday cake or you got the long or short end (it depended on your personal cultural myth) of the wishbone or you dropped pennies into a wishing well. Then we all waited for our wishes to materialize. When they didn't, we became sophisticated and worldly wise and cynical—until the next time.

The only difference between kids and adults is that we adults don't go through all the ritual in wishing. We still wish and wish and wish. None of the wishing ever makes anything come true.

Perhaps the problem many of us have with faith is that we don't really understand the difference between wishing and having faith. Wishing is seeing something and wanting it to be so. Nobody has promised us we can have it. In fact, we have no right to expect to get anything for which we wish. But having faith is believing in a promise. The one who promises is the eternal God who is trustworthy in all things.

With that in mind, think about what the writer of Hebrews said when he described faith. He made two claims about faith: It is substantial, and it is evidence. Both terms describe a concreteness which we rarely relate to something as nebulous as faith.

That is just the point. Faith is not nebulous. Faith is the reality which we hold now about something that is still around the corner. In fact, faith is the evidence, the proof, that what is around the corner is really there.

Take a moment to remember with your mate some of your childhood wishes and how they changed as you grew up. Name together one of God's promises and discuss how that promise may affect your future together.

Pray together, asking God to help you depend on his promises alone.

Week 4, Day 3
THE LIFE-STYLE OF CHRISTIANS
Read Romans 1:16-17

Life-style is a popular word. It describes the way in which we spend our time, the kinds of amusements we choose, the living arrangements we consider necessary. In short, it describes the way we live. The crucial part of all of this is that life-styles can be subject to whims of style. For some people, any fad that is in vogue brings on new life-styles.

Particularly dangerous for Christians is the temptation to let fads and trends determine our life-styles. When we become followers of the world instead of followers of God, we become world-oriented instead of God-focused. The result is obvious. When your life-style is controlled by what is going on in the world around you, your life can become chaotic. That is what is happening to a lot of people today.

The answer is that you've got to choose a life-style which has lasting values and which is focused on God. The Bible puts it this way, "The righteous will live by faith" (Rom. 1:17). This verse applies to much more than your initial decision for Christ. Salvation is no more a mechanical thing than is a vital marriage.

Would you believe it if someone told you that love was just for getting married and wasn't really needed after? Of course not. Just as love is a continuing essential in marriage, so faith is absolutely vital in our life with God. We don't graduate from faith to something better. We keep living in faith and by faith because there is no other way for us to live as God's children.

Faith is our life-style. It is permanent, predictable, and costly. Not costly in the same way that the life-styles of the world are costly, but in the way we must give ourselves to it.

Take a moment to describe together your life-style. If you took Romans 1:16-17 seriously, what changes would you make in your present life-style?

Pray, acknowledging to God that you do not want to be "up on the latest," unless the "latest" is of his doing.

Week 4, Day 4
LIKE A GREEN TREE
Read Jeremiah 17:7-8

Just outside the window of our den is a tree. Someday it is going to be a large, beautiful, shade-giving tree. Right now it is still trying to overcome a near-fatal beginning. Because our growing time in Denver is shortened by severe winters, a good start is important. Knowing this, we were determined that each tree would get plenty of water. We almost drowned that one! Water is important to a growing tree, but the amount of water is also vital.

People are like plants—they grow! Sometimes they get an inadequate diet of that which sustains life, and it shows. They are easily overcome by circumstances. They show little growth though they try. They are just not very effective. But there are those whose growth is steady and healthy. What's the difference? The diet.

A person who trusts in the Lord is like a tree planted close to a water source. The tree is able to reach out and nourish itself just as it needs. The result of this is a lack of fear and worry. If you were a tree, what would be your concern? Obviously, you would be concerned about whether your leaves would be green and whether you were fruitful.

When you are residing in the Lord, you are becoming all that you can be. The unique person that God created in you is being fully and effectively developed. You don't fear the circumstances, and you don't worry about yourself.

Just as a tree doesn't have to be concerned about green leaves and fruit when it is close to its source of nourishment, you don't have to be focused on yourself when your confidence is in the Father.

Take time to share some of the worries you have about yourselves. Then discuss what you can do to help one another depend more on God's nurture.

Pray, asking the Father to forgive you for looking at yourselves so long that you've worried every leaf off. Then ask him to help you have faith that he knows what's best for trees and the two of you.

Week 4, Day 5
HE IS DEPENDABLE
Read Luke 18:8

Ever been disappointed in somebody? Perhaps it was a friend who let you down, or a hero or some political figure or a parent, and now the only thing you can think is "I'll never believe in him again." Part of that is the price of growing up and discovering clay feet on otherwise fairly nice people. Part of it is coming to terms with the fact that some folks are undependable. They make promises which they don't even try to keep.

All of our lives we spend time looking for people we can believe in. That's what marriage is all about. It is a commitment to persons we know a little bit, on the chance that they will be dependable. Most of the time they are, but when they aren't we experience a lot of heartache.

True faith always has a trustworthy object of faith. People who are losers consistently pick untrustworthy objects of their trust. They are always disappointed but never surprised. The object of their affections and confidence let them down; but then, the loser says, that object wasn't dependable anyway.

God is absolutely dependable. People who keep on calling on him are not given a deaf ear. That for which they pray may not be given quickly, but he will not put persons off forever. He is dependable.

Think for a moment of the people who have let you down. Were you expecting more than they had promised? Have you found out that you are the kind of person who keeps relying on untrustworthy people? How much trust do people put in you? What is the trust level in your marriage?

Take a moment to talk about how important it is to feel that you can depend on each other. Share ways in which you do depend on each other.

Pray, thanking God that he is always dependable.

Week 4, Day 6
CAN WE KNOW HIS WILL?
Read Proverbs 3:5-6

Inscrutable. That was the word used about the classic movie detective Charlie Chan. No one knew what he was thinking. You've probably met a few inscrutables. It was simply impossible to know what they had on their minds.

God is inscrutable. That is not one of the classic theological attributes of God, but it is fact anyway. Nobody knows what God is thinking. This would not be such a great problem, except that we are supposed to do his will. How are you going to do the will of an inscrutable? How much time have you spent wondering what God's will was and how you could know it? There is a way.

First, you must want his will. He does not reveal his will for people to add to their options. When you get ready to do his will, then you are on solid ground. Second, you must believe that he wants to show you his will. This is the expression of faith in the goodness of God. Third, you must depend on him to show you his will. This means that you wait upon him even as you continue to do the things you must be doing. Fourth, you must give glory to him alone when his will is shown to you.

I suppose it must also be said that you don't fold your hands and sit idly while this is going on. You must play an active role. You must trust in him with all your heart. You must acknowledge him in everything. As much as possible do not depend too much on your own insight and perception. The promise is, "He will make your paths straight." Straight to where? To where he wants you to be. That's how you will know you are doing his will. You will find yourself there.

Share with each other your mental pictures of what would happen if you followed God's will for your marriage. Would life be better or worse? Define for one another how far you are willing to go in the four-step process mentioned above.

Pray, asking the Father to help you use less time trying to figure out the inscrutable and more time just trusting him.

Week 4, Day 7
PERFECT PEACE
Read Isaiah 26:3

Do you know how dangerous it is to trust in something which cannot bear the load you put on it? When I was a teenager I fancied myself a track star. The area of competition which held my interest for a while was pole vaulting. I built a primitive vaulting pit in our backyard. There was no sand to land in. There were no standards to hold the crossbar. I piled boxes on top of each other with logs set on end at the top. My vaulting pole was a long piece of heavy cane I had bought. The inevitable happened. I was attempting a jump of seven feet and in midair my pole broke. I hit the ground with a thud, and my makeshift standards collapsed on top of me!

Of course, not everything fails like that. You have to decide what can and can't carry the load you have in mind. Once you've tested and are satisfied, you never give it a second thought. Obviously, the more you are able to trust whatever it is you are using or depending on, the less anxiety you will feel.

There are many books in print which are ready to tell you how you can be free from anxiety. The suggested therapies range from the simple to the complex. The Bible has a solution which is simple, tested, and reliable: Find someone who is completely reliable. Of course, that someone is Jesus Christ. He can carry *any* load. Take your worries and your thoughts to him, and leave them in his hands. The result is perfect peace. The best part is that *we* don't give us perfect peace. *He* keeps us in perfect peace.

Share with each other what you are most worried about right now. Also share what effect this worrying has or might have on your relationship.

Pray, asking God to forgive you for overloading yourselves and underloading him. Ask that he help you trust him more and worry less.

Week 5, Day 1
LOVE IS . . .
Read 1 Corinthians 13:4

For the next several days we are going to concentrate on a part of 1 Corinthians 13. You are probably quite familiar with it, but I want you to think very specifically about some of the things which are said to be or not to be expressions of love. You will have to keep in mind that the word for *love* which the Bible uses is one which is natural to God but not so to us.

With that in mind, look first at what love is. Love is patient and love is kind. Big deal! Everybody knows that love is patient and kind. But how patient? And what manner of kindness is being spoken of here?

Older translations of the Bible captured the flavor of it with an old-fashioned expression: "suffereth long." That immediately puts love into a different context. Instead of picturing a good-natured grandpa smiling as he waits for his grandchildren to toddle out to him, we picture anguish, choosing to endure what we do not want to endure. This kind of patience is choosing to keep on holding on when what we really want to do is to let go and run away. When one partner breaks the spirit or the letter of the marriage covenant, love holds on. It's not natural, but it is the way God loves and wants us to love.

Kindness sometimes looks too much like a Norman Rockwell painting. It seems one-dimensional. In reality kindness is a choice of how we relate to people. We can choose to overpower, we can choose to manipulate, or we can choose to serve. Kindness is the choice to serve. Kindness is a decision to be open and vulnerable where assertiveness and aggression are concerned. Kindness is not negotiated. It is a choice which is made before the response can be known.

Talk with one another about the ways patience and kindness have been a part of your relationship, and discuss ways in which you hope they will continue to show up in your marriage.

Pray, thanking the Father for his patience and kindness, and asking him to help you love his way.

Week 5, Day 2
LOVE IS NOT . . .
Read 1 Corinthians 13:4-5

Love *is* some things. Love is also *not* some things. The things love is not are proud, rude, self-seeking, and easily angered. No argument. Except that often we are proud, rude, self-seeking, and easily angered.

The problem, of course, is self. Let's use *myself* as an example. Nobody pays enough attention to me, so I am proud, rude, self-seeking, and easily angered. Sure enough, each one of these gets me a lot of attention. Maybe not the kind of attention I would prefer, but attention does put me back in the limelight.

When a person falls in love one of the easiest things in the world is to step out of the limelight—as long as the person I love keeps pushing me back into the limelight. We are willing to set self aside, but only conditionally. The moment he or she quits making me the center of attention, then I find myself becoming proud, rude, self-seeking, and easily angered again.

Love is not the problem. *Self* is the problem, and loving means both a willingness and a decision to set self aside. Unfortunately, I can be easily fooled into thinking I have set self aside when, in fact, all I have done is to take myself temporarily out of the limelight. Then I expect you to insist that I step right back in. The intrusion of self is very sneaky.

I can also help by being aware that, whenever I become rude, proud, self-seeking, or easily angered, love has silently slipped away to some dark corner. I must be careful not to be tempted into thinking that I can force myself not to be proud, rude, and so forth. I can't. In fact, the more I think about myself not being those things, the more easily I will slip into them. Why? Because *self* is my focus.

I must learn to focus on you as the one who is loved and on the Father who teaches me how to love.

Take a moment to remember and share the times and ways in which you have felt loved by your mate.

Pray, asking the Father to help you focus so much attention on him that his love can flow through the two of you.

Week 5, Day 3
LOVE DOES NOT . . .
Read 1 Corinthians 13:4

Lovers don't blow their own horns or sing their own praises. The proof of that is how quickly people change in their attitude toward those who talk about themselves. In the first blush of love, that type of ego worship may seem cute. We are so enthralled that we want to know everything about the other. After we have been around him or her for a while, fascination turns to boredom. How boring it is to listen to someone who talks only about himself! If he would only forget himself for just a moment! Love directs people's attention away from themselves.

Love also does not envy. But perhaps the word *envy* is too pale and unthreatening. *Jealousy* would capture the meaning best. Love is not jealous. Impossible! Even God is described as jealous. The only couples I know who are not jealous are the ones who are trying to stay away from each other.

Think of jealousy as an attempt to possess another person rather than a response to a broken covenant. A jealous person cannot stand for one's mate to have anything better or anything at all apart. It is an attempt to make the mate live for self alone or have no personal life at all. That is the picture of idolatry. We want to be worshiped as gods in the eyes and minds and affections of our mate.

Like all idolatry, jealousy is destructive. Only God as God has the privilege of being jealous. Because our natural love for each other is an expression of our need, it must constantly be tempered by the kind of love that is not jealous or possessive.

Enumerate together those situations in which you might feel jealousy or the need to have all your mate's attention. What need do you have in each situation that you are willing to express now?

Pray, asking the Father to help us love as he loves, without the need to possess or smother.

Week 5, Day 4
LOVE KEEPS NOT . . .
Read 1 Corinthians 13:5

Love forgives and forgets, but people don't. There are a couple of reasons why. First, nobody really ever forgets anything. Everything that ever comes across our lives is stored somewhere in the gray recesses of our brains. Second, nobody likes to run out of ammunition if there is a chance that there will be a fight.

Because most couples fight at some time or another, you'd better keep your ammunition handy and your powder dry. Some folks feel that, if they don't keep old bruises and wounds and betrayals in a handy ready-to-use place, they will be defenseless. So they keep score on each other.

Love doesn't keep score. It is true that no one can really forget anything. But it is one thing to be aware of wrongs and another to keep score of them, dragging them out for battle once in a while.

Perhaps the problem is that we do not understand what forgiveness is. Forgiveness is not some mechanical procedure by which things are set straight, and we guarantee never to be bothered by that particular matter again. Forgiveness is an act of will to refuse to use the issue at point against your mate now or in the future.

A friend told me about a young woman who could not get rid of her guilt. She kept a long score against herself. Her pastor had her write out her list of sins. Then they shredded and burned the paper. As they watched the flames, he quoted the passages from the Bible which promise God's forgiveness.

If he hides our sins behind his back and sees them no more, why do we drag them out to use against one another? If he is faithful and just to forgive us our sins, and to cleanse us, why do we insist on countermanding his action?

Take time to confess to one another some resentment you would rather not keep. Then covenant together to keep your relationship clear of remembered wrongs.

Pray, asking God to let your forgiveness be longer than your memory.

Week 5, Day 5
LOVE'S DELIGHT
Read 1 Corinthians 13:6

Ever play *vacuum cleaner?* No, you don't crawl around the floor making noises and bumping into the furniture! And vacuum cleaner is neither a children's game nor a new party game. A more common name for this pastime is *gossip*, picking up dirt and then dumping it on somebody.

Love doesn't play vacuum cleaner. The reason is that love, by nature, does not enjoy the bad. Love delights in the truth.

Because we are human, we are more drawn by bad news than good. The public media recognizes this tendency in us and, consequently, news programs provide a catalog of violence, mayhem, and treachery. This tendency becomes personalized when we think the worst of someone we say we love. How long has it been since you firmly rejected someone's attempt to give you the real lowdown about somebody?

Love sees others and accepts them for who they are while refusing to condone the wrong they do. Love yearns for the image of God in everyone.

Take time to share with each other the objects of your delight. What do you enjoy doing and seeing and thinking about? Be truthful. Does the time you spend indicate that the things you identified really are your source of delight? Is it even possible that you secretly laughed and felt smugly satisfied when your partner attempted something and failed? Do you feel you are called by God to keep your partner from getting a swelled head? As you discuss these things, remember that lovers do not delight in evil.

Pray, thanking God for giving you worth and for treating you as worthy of his love, even when you are not. Then ask him to help you see the worth in one another, even when you don't like what the other is doing.

Week 5, Day 6
LOVE ALWAYS . . .
Read 1 Corinthians 13:7

Have you ever heard someone say something positive about hate or negative about love? I don't mean an adolescent phrase like "I positively hate you!" Love is positive. Hate is negative. People feel a plus in love. They feel a minus in hate. Love causes you to look out and look for. Hate causes you to run away or push away.

Lovers are basically positive people. They protect, trust, hope, and endure because love always protects, always trusts, always hopes, and always endures.

Because it is more natural for us to need instead of love, our desire to have our needs met sometimes corrupts the positive aspects of love. If we put our own needs first, then it is easy for protection to become grasping and smothering; trust becomes blind gullibility; endurance becomes masochism. Love is never any of these.

Love protects when protection is needed, not when you need to protect to prove your need to love. Love trusts as a way of being involved and responsible toward one another, not as a way of escaping commitment and responsibility. Love hopes because it is always a covenant with a future, not a way of manipulating a bad penny into a good one. Love endures when misunderstanding and hurt invade the relationship because the relationship is worth the hurt, not because your whole life depends on one other person.

Take a moment to share how important it is for each of you to feel the protection, trust, hope, and endurance of the other. Make a new commitment to each other to come closer to showing these qualities always.

Pray, asking the Father to help you never to give up on one another, as he has never given up on you.

Week 5, Day 7
LOVE NEVER . . .
Read 1 Corinthians 13:8

Your life together will be filled with warranties. Every appliance you purchase will be accompanied by a warranty. Some will be very elaborate. Many will be utterly useless. In fact, the ones which are most impressive are often the least reliable. A warranty is only as good as the willingness and ability of the seller to stand behind his merchandise.

Someday, just before I decide to buy something, I hope to hear a salesperson say, "Of course, you realize that this product is made to last only two years. Any time of use beyond that would be remarkable." When that happens I believe I may be ready for heaven.

Love never fails. That is one warranty which is absolutely secure. Love never breaks down, never quits working, never stops loving, never reaches the point where it no longer functions. Lovers do. But love doesn't. Love will never stop because God is love.

Sadly, the love that many people give seems not to have this never-fail warranty. Their kind of love is an expression of their need. When their need is no longer there, their kind of love no longer lives. Unless your love is disciplined and balanced by God's love, you will not have a dependable warranty.

Remember how easily you spoke your forever vows? At that moment you were certain you would never want to live without each other. But that certainty can fade with the change of emotions. It is then that you understand the importance of vows that commit you to the kind of love that never fails. That is God's kind of love.

Each mate take a moment to visualize what your marriage would be like if you did not need each other. What would be left? Talk together about that dimension of your relationship that is apart from need.

Pray, asking God to make each of you instruments of his love, which never fails.

Week 6, Day 1
LEARNING TO TALK RIGHT
Read Psalm 19:14

I remember how long we worked with our children to help them to speak their first words. Now, when I see my long-distance phone bill each month, I wonder if we overtrained them! To teach someone to use his mouth to form words and give definition to the images of his mind does not guarantee that he will always use that equipment to say words which are acceptable. Remember the taste of soap when you used some of those "new" words the big boys were using so hilariously?

We not only have to learn how to talk; we have to learn to talk right. Talking right means using the right words at the right time to accomplish the right purpose. If you are bothered by all that talk of *right*, use the word *correct* and you will get the same message.

Dialogue means conversation between two people. A lot of so-called dialogue is really a succession of monologues. But dialogue is not enough in a developing relationship. Let me invent a new word which describes the kind of talking which is needed in a healthy relationship: *agapelogue*. To me *agapelogue* means the interchange of words which are formed and expressed and received in that special kind of love which characterizes the mind and heart of God.

Today's Bible verse tells us how to learn *agapelogue*: "May the words of my mouth and the meditations of my heart be pleasing in your sight, O Lord."

Share together those words in your conversations and confrontations that give you trouble. Also share those desirable words you can find to replace those troublesome words.

Pray, acknowledging to the Father that he has taught you how to speak to him, and asking him to teach you also how to speak to one another.

Week 6, Day 2
THAT'S NOT WHAT I SAID!
Read Proverbs 18:13

My mouth occasionally stretches to correspond to a 9 D. That's my shoe size. The reason, of course, is that involuntary reflex which impels my foot into my mouth as soon as my mouth opens to say something. This most often occurs when I get tired of waiting for someone to get through saying what they are saying, and I finish the sentence for them.

I will never forget the embarrassment which flooded my whole being one time when I pulled just such a stunt. I was greeting people one beautiful Sunday morning. The ritual called for an inquiry about a person's state of being. I was assuming they would respond in the proper fashion by assuring me that all went well. My closing of the ritual was a hearty "That's wonderful!" Everything went smoothly until I boomed my closing blessing to a particular man. My mind suddenly started sending frantic signals. He had not said he was doing fine. He had said quite the contrary. After extricating my foot from my mouth I tried to make amends. It was a limp performance.

How much grief and frustration could be avoided if we learned never to answer until the sender has completed his message! Maybe we ought to go back to speaking to each other over C.B. channels. Because both of you have to be on the same channel, both can't talk at the same time. Such a practice may help many of us get out of our bad habits of not really listening.

How many of you and your mate's misunderstandings occur because of a violation of this verse? How often do you see the hurt in someone's eyes because you have stomped in to answer prematurely or take over a conversation? People who don't listen don't really care about others.

Agapelogue means listening as well as speaking. For today, promise yourself that you will listen before you speak. Really listen!

Individually make a list of the occasions in which you feel you are not being listened to. Share these occasions lovingly and carefully. Decide on some signals you can use to let each other know when this is happening.

Pray, asking God to help you to really listen before you answer.

Week 6, Day 3
LEARNING TO LISTEN
Read James 1:19

Have you ever thought what it would be like to drive a car if you could not read the road signs? Not only would you not be able to know where the food, gas, and rest stations were; you would not know when to stop, when to slow down, or when to watch out for hazardous road conditions. In other words, if you could not *listen* to the road signs, you would be in a heap of trouble.

Reading and listening both serve a common function: to bring to our attention the information which is being relayed to us. The difference is that we know we have to look at the *messenger* when we read. But when we *listen* to a speaker, we often just lend him our ears. To really listen you have to pay attention to the one who sends the message, and the best way to pay attention is to look right at the messenger.

There is another thing about listening that I would like for you to know. Listening is not just an activity that is essential to gathering information; it is the main way in which we let people know they are important. Paying attention is a very personal compliment. It is important even when there is no information being shared.

One of the reasons God invites us to pray is so that we will know that he pays attention to us. In a relationship that is healthy most talking is a way of staying in touch, and listening is the way in which people who are staying in touch pay attention to one another.

When a teacher or a parent says, "Pay attention," it is a command to tune in or else. Marriage partners rarely demand attention that explicitly, but the need is even greater. More than simple information is in the balance; the health of a relationship is in question.

"Be quick to listen."

Take turns listening and feeding back what you have heard your mate saying as each of you shares an important event of the day.

Pray, thanking the Father for listening to you when you pray, and asking him to teach you to listen to each other when you speak.

Week 6, Day 4
WELL, SHUT MY MOUTH!
Read Psalm 141:3

Did you ever say something which you knew immediately was totally inappropriate? Do you remember how you wished you could breathe in hard enough to suck all those dumb words back inside you, but you couldn't? Words are powerful, and they are forever. Some scientists have indicated that with the proper equipment, words which were spoken years ago could be picked off of walls and rocks and heard again. Aren't you glad that we don't have such equipment available yet and those dumb words can just lie there? Of course, they don't just lie there. They were heard by someone, and they are imprinted on someone's brain and have carved a hurt on someone's heart. They can never be erased.

The person who coined the cliché "Sticks and stones may break my bones, but words will never hurt me" must have lived his life in perpetual isolation. Words do hurt, and some words ought never to be spoken.

One of the disturbing phenomena in our society is the battered family. It is almost impossible to believe that people could ever do to one another the terrible things which are reported. But people who would never lift a hand batter others with violent words. Some words should never be spoken.

Today's verse takes very seriously the problem of inappropriate words. "Set a guard over my mouth, O Lord; keep watch over the door of my lips." In other words, I need all the help I can get to shut my mouth. I need supernatural help to button loose lips and a flapping tongue.

In Philippians 4 Paul described the peace of God as a guard standing watch over our hearts to keep everything harmful out. In today's verse the psalmist saw God as a guard to keep everything harmful in. There are some words I do not need to speak. There are some words I ought not to speak. There are words I must not speak.

Take time to recall for your mate those words you have regretted in your relationship.

Pray, asking the Father to help you never again say harsh words you will regret.

Week 6, Day 5
THAT LITTLE OLD TONGUE
Read James 3:1-12

Several summers ago there was a period of weeks when our beautiful Rocky Mountains were obscured by smoke. There was a fire in the foothills, raging out of control, and those of us who lived in Denver could not see the western skyline that so dominated our lives. Instead we saw smoke in the daytime and fire at night. We learned later that it had been started by some children playing with fire in their own backyards. From very small sparks, great forest fires grow.

James, in his epistle, described how the tongue, small as it is, can be as destructive as a spark which sets a forest ablaze. He made several statements which appear to be extreme, but upon reflection they are completely accurate. The tongue corrupts the whole person. It sets the whole course of a person's life on fire. A person can tame even the wildest beast, but not the tongue. The tongue can do that which neither tree nor spring can do. They must produce only one kind of fruit or water; but the tongue can both curse and praise.

I recall hearing of a pastor who, harassed by a church member who would not discipline her gossiping ways, accused her of having a tongue which was hinged in the middle so that it could flap at both ends! Hardly a temperate remark, but haven't all of us known persons who have destroyed other people and corroded relationships because they could not or would not bridle their tongues? Isn't it sad that the same tongue which whispers a prayer, sings a lullaby, and licks an ice cream cone is also the one which lashes out in hatred?

Together make two lists: one list of words that spread good feelings through your relationship, and another list of words that spread bad feelings through your relationship. Talk about how certain words can be very powerful.

Pray, thanking the Father for making your tongue to praise him and to tell others of your love for one another. Ask him to help you to use it for that purpose.

Week 6, Day 6
BUILDING WITH WORDS
Read Ephesians 4:29

Love is not something you fall into or out of. I'm not sure what you call that, but I have an idea it is more glandular than anything else! Love is something you make happen as you build it day by day. Like a building, you can tear down love or build it up.

The materials you use in building love are familiar. *Attitudes* are important; *consistent actions* are essential; *faithfulness* is vital; *dependability* is necessary; and *words* are crucial. Most of us understand that the kinds of attitudes, actions, faithfulness, and dependability which are necessary are the positive kinds. No one would dare build a marriage with bad attitudes or quasifaithfulness. You might as well construct the Empire State Building with masking tape and matches!

But do we understand the value of words? Do we understand what they do to a relationship? Some words build it up. Some words can wreck it. In writing to the Ephesian Christians Paul urged them to be careful about the way they talked to each other. The deciding factor was to be the needs of others. The words they were to use were to be those which built others up.

The quickest conclusion that some might have to such instruction is that we are to be long-faced or to constantly hover over each other, keeping a watchful eye out for any disturbance. However, if the needs of others is the criterion for our choice of words, there is a place for all kinds of words: healing words, humorous words, loving words, confronting words. Paul did not mean that we never use words which are disturbing; instead, we never use words as weapons to hurt and destroy others.

Recall to each other those things that have been said by your mate that resulted in your personal growth. It may have been affirmation—it may have been confrontation. It built you up.

Pray, acknowledging to the Father that you really do get far too concerned about yourselves. Your words show it. Ask him to help you to get outside of your shells and become aware of each other's needs.

Week 6, Day 7
HOW TO HEAL
Read Proverbs 16:24

We began this week by coining a new word: *agapelogue*. It means the interchange of words which are formed, expressed, and received in that special kind of love which characterizes the mind and heart of God. As we read the New Testament we see these kinds of words used especially in the conversations of Jesus.

The Old Testament also has some reminders about appropriate words. "Pleasant words are a honeycomb, sweet to the soul and healing to the bones." What a privilege! What a responsibility! Not many of us think of ourselves as healers; but there is a therapeutic quality in words.

Think of all the words which might bring healing in the life of someone you know and love: "I love you." "I am proud of you." "What do you think?" "I am sorry." "Forgive me." "We." There are many more, but each has the quality of fulfilling the specific need for healing at the moment.

What would happen today if you were to use words as instruments of healing? This doesn't mean that you must rack your brain trying to say just the right thing. Instead, just be ready to see each person's need as you meet him or her. The key is *pleasant* words.

So many people are in need of pleasant words! No doubt they are loaded down with the other kinds: critical words, selfish words, attacking words, whining words. But pleasant words are as scarce as hen's teeth.

Start now. Take time to think of five things you feel would be pleasant and healing to your mate. Say them and talk about how good it is to hear healing words.

Pray, acknowledging to the Father that if we didn't have words we couldn't talk to him, and we couldn't know how much he loves us. Then ask him to help you choose your words so that sweetness and healing become a reality.

Week 7, Day 1
HE WHO STEALS MY PURSE
Read Ecclesiastes 7:1

Not many of us would agree with Shakespeare that those who steal our purses steal only trash. That was before credit cards. However, we would agree that those who abuse our names have attacked our last line of defense.

The writer of Ecclesiastes, a realist about everything, says, "A good name is better than fine perfume." Obviously, what he had in mind was more than a name which sounded good. There are a lot of those, but a name doesn't mean much if it is only historical.

I believe there are two important things about good names. First, a good name usually tells something about your family. To come from a family in which strong values are important is something for which to be proud and thankful. To have a name which identifies you as a person whose family is high-minded and trustworthy gives you a good model to follow for life.

Second, a good name is a reflection of who people have come to know you to be. Your family name can only carry you so far. If your own use of that name doesn't carry the load, it won't go very far. What kind of family is represented by your name? Is it one you can bear proudly? More to the point: Is it one which they can be proud you are carrying? None of us lives alone. We are directly linked to three generations: our parents, our siblings, and our children. The name we carry touches upon all three.

Probably the most important is that last generation. Are we living the kinds of lives which will make our children proud to carry our names?

Create together a family motto—a statement that you think accurately portrays what you want your marriage and family to be. Then talk about ways you can live out that motto so that your friends can see it.

Pray, thanking the Father for Jesus, the name above every name, and asking him to help you live so that you will not dishonor any of your names.

Week 7, Day 2
WILL YOU RESPECT ME LATER?
Read Galatians 6:7-10

There is no way to cut yourself off from the consequences of what you do. A great preacher used to say, "Wise men always look to the consequences." There are several ways to interpret that. Perhaps it means that wise men keep second-guessing themselves, or maybe it means that wise men are always looking over their shoulders. I believe that it really means that wise men understand that whatever a person does will have consequences for good or for bad.

People often ignore this truth and live as if there were no tomorrow. But the fact remains: If you get drunk, you have a hangover; if you stuff yourself with candy, you get fat and break out; if you live promiscuously, you . . . well, you get the picture.

There are times when the writers in the Bible make statements which seem extreme. This one may seem that way to you. We tend to think of life in terms of family and long years. But the Bible brings us down to earth: whatever a person does now will have a direct effect on what happens to him later. And there's a further word of advice: We are not to become tired of doing good things. That advice applies to marriages especially.

Today's passage of Scripture focuses on character and poise. Poise is that which enables us to be steady in the midst of life's storms, and character is that which enables others to enjoy the fact that we lived. It is not enough to have as a goal in life the establishing of a dynasty. Too many old cranks have started dynasties.

Take time to share your personal goals for your marriage and family. What do you want for yourselves and your children? Do you and your mate share the same goals? Note any differences the two of you may have, and agree to discuss them in a spirit of love.

Pray, thanking the Father for the gift of possibilities and asking him to help you see the consequences and plan your lives accordingly.

Week 7, Day 3
TREAT ME LIKE A REAL PERSON
Read Proverbs 30:23

When Solomon wrote that a bitter wife is one of the things that would make the earth tremble, perhaps he was responding to something he observed taking place around him. Or perhaps he sadly realized that it is not enough to be married and part of a king's house. There has to be love, even in a king's house.

Unless there is love, marriage is a mockery. It pretends to be something it isn't. It treats a person as a thing, an object, instead of a person.

Marriage is a contract which limits, but also opens up the possibilities for the persons involved. The reward is in the personal growth which takes place when love is growing and vital. A person who is loved is the freest person in the world. A person who is not loved is the most imprisoned. When you combine the limits of the marriage contract with the coldness of not being loved, it is like being shackled to your worst enemy.

Solomon did not say that an *unloving* woman who is married causes the earth to tremble, but a married woman who is unloved is an earthquake-maker. Her needs are neither being recognized nor met. She is the cook, the maid, the laundry woman, the wet nurse, the children's caretaker, even the one used for sexual satisfaction, but she is not seen as a person. When that is true her anger is enormous and it is justified! What kind of man traps a woman and then proceeds to kill her slowly by not loving her? The same is true for the wife.

Husband and wife, take time to let your mate share with you what her/his needs are. Before anything else, your partner is a person and your mate. Your love, undivided and undying, is what he/she must have.

Each of you close your eyes and visualize your mate outside of the daily roles such as vocation, hobby, or mate. What do you see? Share what you see with one another.

Pray, expressing your thanks to the Father for making persons, and asking him to help you to respect each other as God's gift.

Week 7, Day 4
MY FEELINGS ARE IMPORTANT
Read Job 12:1-3

There are several things about the Book of Job which you must know if you are to appreciate the verses indicated for today. Job was an extremely wealthy man. He was called the greatest man among all the people of the East. He was also blameless and upright in his conduct. As the result of Satan's challenge to God, Satan is allowed to do anything to Job except take his life. Such a bargain seems atrociously unfair to our modern ears, but it sets the stage for the most magnificent story in history about how a man deals with the suffering and tragedy which he does not deserve.

Everything happens to Job. He loses everything but his wife, who does little to comfort him, and his friends, who do everything to comfort him—but all wrong! They refuse to accept his plight as undeserved, and they urge him to confess all. They do not take seriously his plea that he cannot understand why this has come upon him. At every turn they discount him and his feelings of frustration and anger.

Finally, he has had enough. "I'm no dummy," Job says. "I can understand all these things you seem to think only you can understand. Quit treating me like a baby. I am a man and I don't understand why this is happening, and neither do you."

Job also speaks for all of those who are caught in circumstances and whose spouses or friends condescend to counsel. To love someone means that we do not treat him as unreal; nor do we treat his feelings as unreal. A true friend is willing to stand by and be silent, to weep or share a laugh. But friends don't lecture each other. And marriage partners must be friends to one another.

Recall together those times and circumstances in which either or both of you spoke down to the other as if he/she were incapable. Talk about the feelings you experienced when you were on the receiving end of such an attitude.

Pray, asking the Father to forgive you when you play god, and thanking him that he has given comfort to you in the person of your mate.

Week 7, Day 5
THE MOST IMPORTANT WORDS
Read Romans 14:13

Do you live with somebody who missed a career as an Olympic diving or gymnastics judge? You know the kind: He or she is always giving you a 7 or a 3 or a -4 in any endeavor. Whenever that person is around, you get so nervous that you stand in danger of cutting your fingers off trying to do a simple job like peeling the potatoes. The next time it happens, hang a potato peel on each of his ears and just keep on going!

We don't have any right to be passing judgment on each other about things which do not matter. This passage is not talking about being convicted about important issues, but the terrible habit we have of constantly measuring people to see if they are our size or do things as we do them. It shows itself in second-guessing other people; finishing the jokes or correcting their stories; or improving on their efforts by priceless pearls of wisdom.

People who love one another do not pass judgment on one another. They do not need to in order to bolster their own ego. Their attitude is one of respect. To respect a person is to see him exactly as he is and to value him fully as a unique person. We don't know enough to judge one another.

People do not need to have every act tested, but to have *who they are* accepted fully. Respect given fully and freely allows a person to blossom into a someone beautiful. The most attractive people are never those who rely on some outward beauty, but those who are loved and respected. They show it. People like that radiate.

Each of you think for a few moments about one behavior of your mate that is irritating to you. Name it to your mate and share what you think would happen if you chose not to be irritated by it anymore, and accept your mate's behavior.

Pray, asking the Father to help you accept one another as he accepts you.

Week 7, Day 6
A LITTLE CONSIDERATION, PLEASE
Read 1 Peter 3:7-8

This kind of Scripture passage is a real bell ringer! It is the kind which awakens any latent feminism in almost any woman. Weaker partner, indeed! Well, before you rip this page out of the Bible and assign Simon Peter a permanent place in the roll call of male chauvinist pigs, put the passage in context. Peter is talking about a certain kind of attitude which enhances a person's spiritual life and witness. For wives he advises the development of inward beauty which is more attractive than any combination of cosmetics. For husbands he advises respect and considerations toward their wives, who stand as equal partners and co-heirs of the gift of grace. The result of this attitude is an unimpaired prayer life.

The most significant factor in this passage is the correlation between husband-wife relationships and effective spiritual growth. We cannot grow spiritually if we do not treat each other properly. We cannot pray as we ought unless we are seeking to be kind and considerate of one another. This makes it imperative that we deal with one another in the best way.

Do you remember when you had trouble praying? Wasn't it because something was in your life which shouldn't have been there? Wasn't it the result of a poor attitude toward someone, so the guilt you were feeling kept you from being able to talk freely to the Father? Prayer is not and cannot be divorced from everything else in our lives. The way we treat one another affects our praying. The attitudes we foster help or inhibit our spiritual growth.

The woman who is growing spiritually is the one who is seeking inward beauty and whose true beauty is manifested in the way she treats her husband. The man who is growing spiritually is the one who is constantly considerate of his wife, giving her the respect she deserves to have.

Recall together some time when your prayers were hindered or you did not feel like praying because of a broken relationship or because you had hurt someone. Share your feelings about that time.

Pray, asking the Father to forgive you for not praying for each other constantly.

Week 7, Day 7
THE GIFT OF PERSONHOOD
Read John 4:7-9

One of the most amazing things about Jesus was the ease with which he could move through barriers. It was a totally unselfconscious type of thing. If it had been forced, even for the sake of something good, the affected persons would have drawn away from him, offended by his intrusion into their personal lives.

His experience with the woman at the well gives several clues. She was a much-married woman, now living with a man without benefit of ceremony. She was a person with whom no proper people would have dealings. She was a Samaritan, a national group with which no self-respecting Jew would have dealings. She was a woman, and Jewish men did not publicly interact with any women.

Jesus came to her as a helpless person needing a favor: a drink of water for a tired and dusty traveler. Her response was a natural reflex: "How come you are violating all the codes?" Perhaps there was a playful sarcasm, or perhaps it was her way of coping with what life had dealt to her. He answered in kind. The conversational tone quickly changed. She had been drawn into an awareness of two miracles. The first miracle was the transformation which Jesus offered her. The second miracle was the gift of personhood. She moved from being victimized by life into seeing herself as one who was truly loved and fully a person.

We are not in a position to do the things Jesus did; but those who know him are in the possession of a gift which he enables them to pass on: the gift of personhood. Do you give that gift every day? Does your partner know that you have given such a gift to him or her?

Each of you make a list of three situations in which you feel most inadequate. Take turns sharing these. When your partner has shared, affirm him/her without conditions.

Pray, asking the Father to help you affirm one another as Jesus affirmed the Samaritan woman.

Week 8, Day 1
NOBODY KNOWS THE TROUBLE I'LL SEE
Read Luke 22:33

For the next several days we will be watching one of the most fascinating people in history during his darkest moment. Part of the problem was the circumstances in which he found himself; but most of the problem was due to his overestimation of his own strength. The man, of course, is Simon Peter. The moment was the dark night of his denial of Christ.

Many things about Simon are attractive. He was a very open person. Whatever he felt he blurted out! He was also given to extreme statements and judgments. He was also prone to making promises he could not keep.

That's where most of us get into trouble. We think every day will be like today, and we assume that we will always be *up* to the challenge. There's no problem as long as the challenges remain in our heads; unfortunately, life involves other people who can bring unbelievable pressure to bear on us. We can in a moment have all our expected support swept away. In the twinkling of an eye everything can be changed, and radical changes have a way of leaving us hanging.

None of us can read the future, especially our own personal future. That's why it is so dangerous to make proud promises about what we will and will not do. Such promises are usually made in our own strength with never a prayer for God to bear us up when we fail or catch us when we fall.

We need to have more of the attitude of the psalmists, who seemed always to expect the worst and thus constantly cried to God for help. If Simon had caught a little of their spirit, perhaps things would have been different that night.

Take time to talk about your expectations for your own marriage that make it different from all the rest. In what ways is your marriage human and in need of God's help?

Pray, acknowledging that the Father knows all this day holds for you. Then ask him to make you weak enough to need him all day long and strong enough to ask him for help.

Week 8, Day 2
THE INEVITABILITY OF FAILURE
Read Luke 22:34

Death and taxes. Someone has said that these are the only constants in life. You can add to that list one more: the inevitability of failure. Even winners finally lose. During the decade of the 1950s, Bud Wilkinson led the Oklahoma Sooner football teams to unmatched winning strings. But there was a Notre Dame down the schedule somewhere, and even the mightiest team came to a screeching halt!

The fact of this truth should not alarm or depress or excuse us. We are imperfect people living in an imperfect world populated by other imperfect people. Permanent perfection is out of the question. After saying all that, I must admit that I have a hard time losing at anything. My whole world is sometimes wrapped up with the urgent, absolute need to win. I think if I lose, I'll die.

Look at Simon Peter. Failure was already predicted. Peter refused to let himself be counted in with that ragtag bunch of losers. Consequently, his fall was worse than the others; and he hit the ground twice as hard! He would not heed the warnings which Jesus pressed upon him.

Peter's kind of blindness keeps us setting ourselves up for failure. We refuse to read the signs, to hear the warnings; and we are shocked when we suddenly find ourselves doing what we promised ourselves we would never do. We see too dimly our own inadequacies.

A lot of what it means to grow up is coming to terms with ourselves as less than perfect and with the world as less than perfect. It allows us to be gracious to those who stumble and fall, even if that somebody is ourselves.

Take time to share your feelings about failure with one another. Don't be afraid to admit the possibility of failure. That is the only way to really ask for help.

Pray, admitting to the Father that so much of your life and energy are tied up in needing to win. Then ask him to help you know that his love is not tied to your winning and to help you love one another, especially when you fail.

Week 8, Day 3
RESOURCES FOR TEMPTATION
Read Luke 22:46

I hope you have taken the time to read the entire sad story of the events which the Gospels record about that dark night when Peter denied Jesus. Since you know what is going to happen, you may be tempted to try to warn people. You can't do that, of course, but you do want to grab Peter and shake some sense into him! Perhaps the reason we become so indignant with him is because we are so like him.

Things are moving along at a rapid pace. The soldiers are coming. The crowds are rehearsing their cries for crucifixion. The leaders are caught up in their scheming. It is going to happen and, sure enough, Peter is sleeping! The writer tells us that he and the others were worn out from their agony and sorrow. But Jesus knows that what is ahead is worse than what they have passed through. The real test of faithfulness is still ahead. Now more than ever, they are in need of resources to resist temptation.

What are your resources in your struggle against temptation? To have strong memories of what people expect from us is important. A lot of people have extended themselves heroically because they could not disappoint those who expected certain standards. Others have found special resources in fellowship with those going through stresses.

There is one resource which is above all others. It is prayer. Prayer links us with God's power, and he is our unfailing partner when we are struggling with failure and unfaithfulness. Prayer is essential at all times—especially when faithfulness hangs in the balance. God has promised to hear us when we pray and give us what we need. When the tide of events seems to sweep you along and you seem helpless, cry out to him.

Take a moment to share how important faithfulness is. Help each other identify the areas in which temptation is usually hardest to bear. Ask for one another's help in dealing with temptation.

Pray, asking the Father to help you understand how weak you really are and how strong he really is and how much he wants to give you his strength.

Week 8, Day 4
IN THE WRONG PLACE AT THE RIGHT TIME
Read Luke 22:54-55

People who love one another must be faithful. You won't argue with that, I'm sure. But do you realize that as much as you love God, there are times when you are unfaithful to him? You won't argue with that, either! Being faithful to the Father comes twenty-four hours each day. No one can be faithful to anyone every minute of every day! No argument there.

So why do you think you can be absolutely faithful to one another all the time? The reason is the difference in our understanding of faithfulness between ourselves and between ourselves and God. Faithfulness to God means always and everything. But we usually think faithfulness to one another means keeping our vows about sexual faithfulness. We assume that as long as we don't run off with somebody else, we are being faithful. That is a very narrow and inadequate definition of faithfulness. Being faithful to one another means being everything we are supposed to be as spouses. It means refusing to use anything as an escape hatch to run away from one another in times of problems.

Peter had followed Jesus. He wanted to stay as close to Jesus as he could. But he made the mistake of using the enemy's fire to warm himself. He was definitely at the wrong place.

Being at the right place is so important in the struggle to be faithful. The person who exposes himself to temptation is playing with fire. There are times when we cannot choose our places, and the Lord has promised special strength when that is truly the case. But for the person who plays with fire, he only has himself to depend on.

The time you spend together is important for the bonding and strengthening it gives to each of you when you must be apart. The time you spend apart can be a time of continued strengthening if you do not play games with your faithfulness.

Take time to talk about how your time together can make you stronger in being faithful when you have to be apart.

Pray, thanking God for his constant faithfulness. Ask him to help you never to hurt your mate.

Week 8, Day 5
TELL THE TRUTH, DUMMY!
Read Luke 22:56-60

Teenagers characteristically have skin problems. Some break out when they eat chocolate or other sweets; some break out during periods of stress.

I had the strangest case of all. My forehead would give me away when I lied. My mother told me she always knew when I was lying; it was written on my forehead! I wore bangs down to my eyes all the way through high school to keep from giving myself away. It might have been better if I had tried telling the truth.

Picture Peter seated at that fire, trying to look as inconspicuous as possible. The inevitable confrontation came: "He's one of them!"

For a moment, a split second perhaps, he started to tell the truth. But it was easier to lie. It was easier until he had to tell the next one to cover the first, and it really got messy when he had to deny the obvious. By then he was mad at everybody: at the people who *forced* him to lie; at Jesus who got him into this mess; and at himself for being such a dummy!

You've been there, haven't you? We all have. We would give anything if we could start all over again and tell the truth, the whole truth, and nothing but the truth. The ironic thing is that we only feel that way after the fact. Before that first lie we just want to do the best thing for everyone concerned. That means, of course, that we do whatever is necessary to do what we want to do without being hassled.

Little lies are like little worms. Enough of them can strip a tree. Enough little lies can erode trust in a relationship. Most of the time we only tell them so we won't make waves. In no time there is a hurricane blowing. People who love one another want to tell each other the truth in order to keep the trust level high. Speak the truth . . . in love!

Take time for each of you to share what you are willing to do to maintain trust in your relationship. Make a covenant of trust.

Pray, acknowledging to the Father that you have a hard time telling him the truth sometimes, and asking that he help you know what lying does to love and what truth does for trust.

Week 8, Day 6
WHEN ALL THE ROOSTERS CROW
Read Luke 22:61-62

Unfaithfulness has a way of coming to light. We are either found out by others or we are found out by ourselves. Sometimes it is a combination of both.

Poor Peter! Everything happened just the way that Jesus said it would. He had been so predictable! He told the lies. The rooster crowed. Jesus looked at him and there was a great revelation. He was not the big strong fisherman, ready to lop off heads. He was a weak lily-livered coward, too scared to talk straight. "He wept bitterly."

When the roosters crow, it is all over. How many times have you found out the truth of that? In school? In jobs? In relationships?

It is also true that when the roosters crow, it is the chance for a new beginning. Unfaithfulness always carries with it a reckoning time. The rooster is going to crow. But when that time comes there is also the possibility of the kind of response which opens a door instead of nailing it shut.

The full impact of Peter's sin burst upon him, and he gave full expression to the agony of his shame. I doubt that he blamed anybody. People who blame others don't weep bitterly. They just keep on crawfishing from one corner to another. People who weep bitterly are coming to terms with their shame, their sin, and themselves. It is their first big chance.

The moment when the rooster crows can be the most hopeful moment of your life. It can be like a new birth. Those bitter tears can be an echo of the cries of an infant just born. It can be one of the most important moments in your life personally and spiritually.

Take time to share with one another any painful moments of reckoning you remember. Share also the growth it brought. Use this moment to affirm one another. There will be tears, but that is all right. I'm sure Simon never told the story without tears of memory and rejoicing.

Pray, thanking God for the forgiveness that makes you a new person with new chances.

Week 8, Day 7
THE PROMISE OF FORGIVENESS
Read Luke 24:34

We come to the end of a bittersweet story. All four Gospels contain the account of Peter's denial of Jesus. This story must have meant a great deal to the early church because of the amount of space given to it in the Bible. I think there were special reasons for that prominence.

If it could happen to Simon Peter, it could happen to all of them. He had become a spiritual giant, but there was this skeleton in his closet known to all of them. His wound of weakness brought him closer and gave them hope in their own struggles with unfaithfulness.

Another reason for its prominence was the testimony about the power which was available that enabled men to overcome even the worst things in life. Had anyone done anything worse than Peter? Poor Judas had done no worse. If Peter could come back, then anyone could come back. His coming back is one of the most beautiful stories in the Bible.

There is a silence about Peter between the sounds of weeping and early morning sounds on resurrection day. What dark nights of the soul he endured! When the news came from the women about the empty tomb, Peter got up and ran to the tomb, examined the evidence, and went away wondering to himself.

Verse thirty-four sums it all up: "The Lord has risen and has appeared to Simon." Jesus had restored the relationship. He had forgiven Peter.

Forgiven: it is the miracle word which comes from the heart of the Father. It is the Father's favorite word. It is the word he wants us to hear. It is the word he wants us to speak to one another. It is the word that makes faithfulness possible by removing unfaithfulness as far as the east is from the west.

Take time to share how it feels to be forgiven. Talk about why it is so hard to be willing to ask for and accept forgiveness. Think of two things for which you want forgiveness. Ask. Receive. Affirm one another.

Pray: "Father, be merciful to me, a sinner."

Week 9, Day 1
WHAT WE DON'T KNOW CAN HURT OTHERS
Read Luke 23:24

Pilate's appointment as procurator in the eastern area of the Roman Empire was a sign that he did some things better than other men. If the legends about Pilate are half true, he deserves more credit than we give him. Unfortunately, he appeared at a very critical time, and he did not behave very well. For a man who wanted to do everything well, he did nothing well.

Because the Jews intended to get rid of Jesus legally, and because they were powerless to do so, they selected Pilate as the hit man. Only he could give the command to kill Jesus. The only problem was that Pilate could not convince himself that Jesus had done anything worthy of death. "Why?" was his question to the Jews. He frankly did not understand their fanaticism. He could find no fault with Jesus. But he went along. "He decided to grant their request." What he didn't know did not keep him from really hurting Jesus. That is also your problem and mine. It is the sore point in many troubled relationships.

"I didn't mean to," and "I didn't intend to hurt," and "I didn't know I was doing anything that would hurt"—all of these are empty phrases which don't keep us from hurting others or make the hurting any less real. We may plead ignorance, but ignorance does not dry tears or ease aching hearts.

One sign of a maturing relationship is our willingness to be responsible for the consequences of our actions. Even when we don't know, people are hurt. The other side of responsibility is a willingness to be open enough with our partners that they do not have to relate to us in ignorance. This week we are going to think about forgiving. We need to because we hurt each other. Even in ignorance.

Take a moment to talk about how difficult it is to be willing to be responsible for what you do.

Pray, asking the Father to teach you to forgive and forgive and forgive.

Week 9, Day 2
THE STUMBLING BLOCK
Read Mark 11:25

The old man lay dying. The pastor, in an effort to help him approach death, asked him about his spiritual life. Was there anyone against whom he held a grudge? "No," came the feeble answer. Were there no enemies he needed to forgive or ask forgiveness from? Again he answered, "No."

The pastor could hardly believe that this old and cantankerous person could have lived without making enemies. He pushed a little harder. Were there no enemies made during his lifetime? Now the old man cackled with glee. Of course there had been enemies, but he had outlived every one! That's hardly the proper way to take care of forgiveness.

Asking for forgiveness is not a way of getting away with something or getting by. Forgiveness is directly related to the health of relationships, and healthy relationships include ours with the Father. Unforgiveness causes blocks in our spiritual lives. We suffer spiritual laryngitis so that we are not able to speak to the Father. We have spiritual blocks so that we keep forgetting what it is we want to ask him. We keep showing up at the altar of prayer with bloody shins where we have been tripping over the stumbling blocks of an unforgiving heart and an unforgiven neighbor.

You cannot carry burdens into the Father's presence if you don't intend to hand them over. You cannot open your hands to receive his blessings if they are clenched around your gunny sack of grudges. Our fellowship with the Father ebbs and flows according to our readiness to forgive.

Take time for each of you to answer this question: Do you have a gunny sack in which you have been storing all those wrongs which others have done to you? Open it up right now and let them all crawl out of your life and heart and mind. Share them with your mate. Forgive each person. Ask the Father to help you. Forgiveness is not easy.

Pray, asking the Father to help you get over the difficulty of forgiving people for what they have done to you.

Week 9, Day 3
THE KEY TO THE DOOR OF LOVE
Luke 7:36-50

Do you have any keys you no longer use? You know, the keys to old cars, old doors, old lockers. It seems silly to keep things which you can no longer use. Do you have some doors for which you don't have keys? That's probably even sillier.

This week we are thinking about the importance of forgiveness in a growing relationship. People who love one another forgive one another because forgiveness is the key to the door of love. That is what Jesus was trying to teach Simon, the Pharisee.

Invited to Simon's house, Jesus was approached by a woman who proceeded to wet his feet with her tears, wipe them with her hair, and pour perfume on them. Her extravagant demonstration embarrassed Simon, who knew what kind of life she had lived. Simon also felt that if Jesus were a truly spiritual leader, he would both know her character and reject her because of it.

Jesus knew what Simon was thinking and took the opportunity to tell a story about debt and forgiveness. A man was owed money by two different men, neither of whom could repay. One sum was ten times the other. He forgave them both. Then Jesus asked the question, "Which of the two will love him more?" The answer was obvious. The greater the sense of forgiveness, the greater the love that flows out to the forgiver.

It is important to remember that Jesus was not saying that we easily forgive those we love the most—forgiveness is always hard—but that *we love most those who forgive us most.* In a love relationship forgiveness must be a consistent and vital reality, or love dries up. People who love one another forgive one another so that they might keep loving.

Take time to answer these questions for one another. What difficulties do you experience with forgiveness? Is it harder for you to forgive or accept forgiveness?

Pray, acknowledging to the Father that he has forgiven you so much that you can never love him enough, and asking him to teach you about love and forgiveness between one another.

Week 9, Day 4
HOW MANY TIMES MUST I FORGIVE?
Read Matthew 18:21

Barefoot boy with cheeks of tan. That might be a good description of Simon Peter except for one omission: barefoot boy with cheeks of tan and foot-shaped mouth! It seems that every time he opened his mouth, Peter's foot rose to the occasion. This question is an excellent example: "How many times shall I forgive my brother?"

Peter may have been immature about many things, but his question reveals that he understood some of the uncomfortable things about forgiveness.

We usually have no problem excusing somebody when he has done us wrong. The one who excuses another's wrongs or rationalizes his antisocial behavior considers himself above that sort of thing. The element that is missing is the one which involves forgiveness: relationship. Where there is no relationship, there is no forgiveness.

A state may pardon a criminal, but it cannot forgive because forgiveness has to do with relationship. Forgiveness is the healing for hurt, pain, and betrayal with the real chance that all of it is going to have to be done again. (We'll talk about that tomorrow.)

When God says he pardons us, he means that all our penalties are canceled in Jesus Christ. When he says he forgives, he is talking as a hurting Father who wants very much to restore a relationship.

Peter's question takes on a lot more meaning and weight. How many times can I forgive if forgiving takes all that? The answer is relationships. How much do you want the relationship, and how easily can you do without it?

Take a moment to share what repeated forgiveness means for you.

Pray, confessing to the Lord that you have a tough time being willing to forgive.

Week 9, Day 5
490?
Read Matthew 18:22

To glance over Jesus' answer to Peter is to misunderstand what it means to really forgive. We must not interpret the demand of Jesus in a sentimental fashion.

We can do the same thing with other stories of the Bible. We think we understand what it means to be an Abraham and have God ask for our son. We think we understand Hosea and what it means to have God push you back into running after a slut of a wife over and over again. We think we understand what it means to forgive the same person for the same offense 490 times. In truth, all of these demands are utterly impossible!

To forgive is to die a little or a lot, depending on what must be forgiven. How many times can a person die a little or a lot? How many times can a person experience betrayal and pain and broken trust and survive?

The work of God is to push us more and more into places where we cannot stand on our own strength. There is nothing which accomplishes this more effectively than being called on to forgive . . . and forgive . . . and forgive.

When we are pushed to the limit, we realize how little we desire to really forgive or how feeble we are at forgiving. It is then that a door opens. It is a door into heaven, and we have an opportunity to call for help. If we do not call out, or if we think that we can do it without God's help, we will probably begin to slowly drift away from that person who needs the healing we alone can give.

Is there someone who needs your forgiveness? Are you willing to confess your feebleness concerning forgiveness? God can help you do that which you cannot do. Even to the point of forgiving 490 times.

Take a moment to make a list of the things which you find nearly impossible to forgive. Be aware of what you are feeling as you read these lists to one another.

Pray, asking the Father to help you to do his work of forgiveness.

Week 9, Day 6
IN FORGIVING WE ARE FORGIVEN
Read Matthew 18:23-35

Sometimes Jesus told stories that stretched people's abilities to believe. Kings in ancient times were as likely to forgive large debts as your local loan shark! Can you imagine what would have happened with other creditors when they learned of this king's kindness?

So the story is not about earthly kings and cash debts. It is about the Heavenly Father who does things which no earthly king would ever think of doing. It is also about how we participate in or block what the King is doing.

The Father forgives for two reasons: it gives him great joy to do so, and it provides hope for us. Whether we realize it or are willing to admit it, our debt is beyond the ability of any of us to repay. However, his forgiveness hinges on our willingness to forgive.

Keep in mind what we've been saying about the true nature of forgiveness. It means that we lose both our claim on the past and the privilege of bringing it up in the future. It is true that in doing so we keep the best of all—God's forgiveness. But we don't feel that way when we are struggling to forgive.

It is such an easy thing to grandly forgive with the lips but not budge an inch in our hearts. How does God know whether we have forgiven or not? He knows because he sees the heart. How do we know he knows? Our attitude always reveals whether we wanted his forgiveness. The person who is just out for himself will never be troubled when he is unforgiving. The one who hungers and thirsts after forgiveness is heartstricken when he realizes what he has been doing to others.

Take a moment to share some things which keep coming back even though you think you forgave long ago. How much longer will you hold on to these memories for your purposes?

Pray, asking the Father to make you a channel of blessing to one another.

Week 9, Day 7
THE HAPPIEST MAN
Psalm 32:1-2

This week we have been thinking together about forgiveness. People who love one another feel compelled to forgive. In the absence of forgiveness there is nothing on which to build a relationship. Loving means listening to one another; but there are times when we are so caught up with ourselves that we don't listen and forgiveness becomes necessary. Loving means giving respect to one another; but there are times when we are so defensive that we dare not be open enough to dignify anyone, and forgiveness becomes necessary. Loving means being faithful in all things; but there are times when we cheat in petty ways, running away to friends or family or hobbies or business, or we cheat in more tragic ways, and forgiveness becomes necessary.

When we are betrayed we die a little. When we forgive we die some more, but it is the only way life is possible. Forgiveness is the way of the cross. But the way of the cross is the only way to enduring life for ourselves and our relationships.

Happy is the man who is forgiven. That is the testimony of the psalmist. Traditionally Psalm 51 is David's agonizing confession of sin and his beggar's cry for forgiveness. Psalm 32 is the testimony of a man (David) who received the promised forgiveness of God. The picture is complete. There is nothing against him, and there are no games being played inside him.

Take time to contrast those times in your relationship when you have felt alienated (unforgiven) and reconciled (forgiven). What feelings did you experience in each?

Pray, confessing your need for forgiveness. Ask the Father to give you a heart ready to forgive.

Week 10, Day 1
SAVED BY GRACE
Read Ephesians 2:8

How much do you know about grace? This week we are going to be thinking about those experiences of life which reveal grace. The hardest part may be in trying to define grace.

First, grace is a gift. This is obvious, but some characteristics about grace are not discernible in other gifts. For instance, gifts are normally exchanged between friends. In grace this is not true. Grace is manifested toward us before we have status as friends before God or even desire any kind of relationship with God.

Now we have something else in the picture—a new dimension which may either complicate or clear up the picture: God.

Grace is a gift from God, but it is his doing for us what we do not deserve. This distinguishes grace from gifts which we might earn by virtue of friendship. Grace is also that which God does for us because we cannot. Grace is divine work, and we are utterly unable to get by any other means that which is given to us freely. The passage for today emphasizes this. We are not only saved by grace, but the very faith which we use to respond to God's gracious offer is itself a gift of grace.

There is a third characteristic of grace which keeps it from becoming humanlike. God not only gifts us with that which we do not deserve and could never get, but he does it in such a way that we do not feel beholden to him. In human gift exchanging, there is an unspoken obligation expected. Everyone knows the feeling of receiving a gift from someone who has a hidden agenda in the transaction.

The word which is most often used with grace is *free*. Grace is free, or it is not grace. When we learn that truth, then we begin to sing songs from our hearts about grace. Until then we keep trying to figure out God's angle in all this giving.

Take time to make a list of four things you have which you do not deserve and have not earned. Share your list with your mate.

Pray, telling the Father that if we really knew what grace was all about, we would never turn off our praise!

Week 10, Day 2
A PROMISE FOR EVERY DAY
Read Deuteronomy 33:25

Do you like garage sales? We had one—once. It was reasonably successful. But when people came at the crack of dawn, I decided maybe I wasn't the garage-sale type. The fascination for garage sale followers is the possibility of finding bargains in the midst of the castoffs.

Sometimes the most precious jewels in the Bible are found in strange contexts. Take this promise, for instance. If your Bible contains any paragraph headings or notes, you are aware that this section contains Moses' last words to Israel. Like an aging father, he has gathered his children around him to bless them. Tribe by tribe, family by family, they hear his words. These specific words are part of the blessing upon Asher. To this obscure figure and his descendants and to us comes the promise of the gracious presence of God every day. "The bolts of your gates will be iron and bronze." That is the promise of the protection of God.

The apostle Paul has much the same idea in Philippians 4 when he promises that the peace of God will guard (do sentry duty) over our hearts if we trust in the Father. Who can break through when the gates are solid and the sentry is never sleeping?

Note the other promise in verse 25: "Your strength will equal your days." How can such a thing be true when we are so aware of our limited strength? Are we made more powerful, or does God manage the days and events to fit our strength? Verse 27 in the KJV says: "The eternal God is your refuge and underneath are the everlasting arms." Can we add anything to that?

Today, I remember one thing: grace. It is the grace of strong gates and everlasting arms! As circumstances arise keep that image in your mind and heart. Meditate on that. Rest upon that.

Share with one another those times in your life when you remember that God's protection was obvious to you. List those things in your relationship which help you feel secure.

Pray, asking the Father for a heart that is willing to rest in him all day long.

Week 10, Day 3
DON'T FORGET THIS PROMISE
Read 1 Corinthians 10:13-14

While Paul spoke much of grace, he was aware that this most precious of doctrines was vulnerable to abuse. In the book of Romans he confronted those who think that an emphasis on grace will lead to immoral living. Anyone who thinks that way doesn't understand grace at all; much less has he experienced it.

The same kind of warning needs to accompany the promise of grace found in today's passage. Temptation is common to us all. In fact, we may be so aware of the power and presence of temptation that we may tend to despair. But Paul reminded us of three truths: 1) no temptation is unique; 2) God in his faithfulness will not let any of us be tempted beyond limits; 3) in each temptation he will provide a way out.

This wonderful promise is effective armor for our daily battles with temptation. It is better than any twenty-four-hour protection system. There are two things, however, which must be noted carefully. The first is the wording of the part of the promise about the way out which God provides. It is not an escape hatch but an ability to stand up under the circumstance. Grace is always grace in the midst of temptations.

The second thing which must be noted is our responsibility where temptation is concerned. No person has a right to wander into lions' dens or fiery furnaces and then expect this promise to operate automatically. At that point we are tempting God, not enduring temptation. The strong suggestion for Christians is "flee." Do not expose yourself to temptation carelessly. It will come unbidden. When that moment comes, remember this Word.

Take time to share some of the sources of greatest need in temptation. Tell your mate how you will help in his or her need.

Pray, asking the Father to help you be aware when you are inviting temptation, to help you accept your weaknesses, and to flee to him.

Week 10, Day 4
WHEN YOU RUN OUT OF STEAM
Read Isaiah 40:27-31

Do you recall the little engine who could? Generations of little achievers have been nourished on the story of the brave little locomotive who overcame hardship by positive thinking. He was not as big as the big streamlined diesels, but he valiantly puffed to the top of the hill. "I think I can . . . I know I can." Those are good words for children trying to adjust to an adult world.

There is a difference, however, in the emphasis which is made by nursery stories and Bible stories. In nursery stories we are led to believe that we can do anything if we just set our minds to it. In the Bible we run right into the wall of reality. There are some hills we cannot climb no matter how hard we puff!

In the Bible stories we are encouraged to take our eyes off of ourselves and put them on God. We are urged to be aware that even the strongest fail. The only unfailing One is the Everlasting God. He will not grow tired or weary. He has grace unlimited and freely available.

The hardest part for us is to see ourselves as needing any help at all. To think of ourselves as not being able to take at least one more step is not tolerable. But "even youths grow tired and weary, and young men stumble and fall."

God's promise is not for permanent youth, but for grace to keep on keeping on no matter what life deals us. Those who hope in the Lord shall renew their strength. Some shall know ecstasy. Some shall know the steady run. Some shall only be able to walk, but they will not faint. Isn't that a better bargain than puffing up the hill? You can run out of steam, but you can't run out of the supply of the grace of God.

Discuss together some of the blessings God has to offer you which could be strength for your marriage when it seems weak or tired.

Pray: "Father, we don't like to think of our marriage as a pooped-out puffer, but the truth is we may sometimes run out of steam. Help us to hope in you, to find strength in you."

Week 10, Day 5
GRACE IS ENOUGH
Read 2 Corinthians 12:7-10

In our attempts to understand God and how he does things, we tend to bring him down to our size. The result is usually a sentimental portrait of one who is so sweetly reasonable that it is impossible to believe that he could have offended anyone.

Sometimes our concept of grace also suffers from sentiment. It needs steel, or it is in danger of becoming a stuffed teddy bear. This passage will take care of that. It is all the steel we need and more than we can stand.

Paul was the victim of something which he called a "thorn in the flesh." We have no clear clues to identify the source of the pain. But imagine a sliver of wood or metal lodged just deep enough to make your finger throb. You can't do anything with that hand. So Paul prayed and prayed and prayed. The Father said no. To get a good picture, think of a small child asking for a painful splinter to be removed. Imagine yourself refusing his request; then see if you can believe you did it all because of love.

Think about that long enough and you start understanding something about the tough-love side of grace. Until you see the tough love in God's grace, you cannot experience the truth of the sufficiency of God. I openly confess that there is nothing harder to believe; nor is there anything which so stabilizes life when you come to believe it.

God's answer to Paul's urgent plea for deliverance was three-dimensional: 1) you need it (the thorn) because you tend to get too big for your britches; 2) you need me more than you need for that thing to be removed; and 3) I can't do what I want to do in your life if you only let me use what you think are your strong points. "My strength is perfected in (not despite) your weakness."

Consider together your own "thorns in the flesh"—for example, something in your past experience that has been painful and did not easily get better. Share your feelings about it.

Pray: "Father, we are scared when we think that there might be some things you are not going to change for us. Please help us to be available for grace to be made perfect in us."

Week 10, Day 6
THAT LITTLE OLD QUILTMAKER
Read Romans 8:28-39

Quilting is coming back, and I'm glad. Years ago, when quiltmaking was more than a fashion, it not only served a social purpose but provided real warmth through the cold months. There were no centrally heated homes and those good, sturdy quilts trapped the body heat in. The true fascination of quilts is the way they are made. Scraps of cloth are blended into beautiful patterns. Little pieces of material that could not be used for anything else are sewn to other little pieces of material, and the result is something very useful. Quiltmaking can teach us how important it is to see the usefulness in things that seem useless.

This is the message of Romans 8:28. "And we know that in all things God works for the good of those who love him." Theologically, this would support the doctrine that God overrules the bad and the good for the purposes of his grace. Practically, it means that God is a quiltmaker. He takes leftovers, rag ends, the useless, even the shameful—and he fashions something beautiful and useful in the lives of those who love him.

That last part is important. Those who don't love him could hardly care less what he is doing. The only thing they care about is their own welfare. Ready-made is more their line. Quilts take too long, and these persons cannot depend on their turning out just to their own taste. But for those who love him, his work is their greatest joy. No matter how long it takes, they know the end result is going to be more beautiful than eye can see, ear can hear, or tongue can describe. When the quilt is finished, no matter what he used, we shall all look like his Son. If that doesn't make a chill run up your spine, you'd better pinch yourself!

Think about your mate for a moment. What is some trait in your mate that he or she thinks is more liability than asset? Tell your mate about that trait you think God uses or can use to fashion something beautiful.

Pray: "O Father: Here are all our 'pieces,' some of which we would rather discard. Take us and make us into your handiwork. Thank you."

Week 10, Day 7
THAT'S ALL I WANT
Read Psalm 23:1-6

I had just come in from driving across one hundred miles of open Oklahoma country. I commented to a friend on how many cows were lying on the ground in the middle of the day. A rancher by trade, he told me that, unless cows are lying down in the middle of the day chewing their cuds, there has to be something wrong.

I thought about the Shepherd Psalm and the part that reads, "He makes me lie down in green pastures." When I mentioned the new insight I had about this old psalm, he informed me that he doubted whether anyone could understand the Bible unless he was a farmer or a rancher!

A little boy learning Scripture misquoted it but caught the truth very effectively: "The Lord is my shepherd, that's all I want." That is the most important fact in all of life. We do not want God because of what he can do for us. We want God for himself, or we do not really want him at all. The things he does for us are because he loves us, not in order to get us to love him. What he does for us takes in every part of life and every circumstance.

Look down at your hand. Each finger stands for a word in the first phrase of the psalm. Your ring finger is the *my* in that phrase. Remind yourself of the great fact of how much you mean to God and how much he means to you by taking hold of that finger. Remember to do that several times today.

You may have wondered why we started this week with Ephesians 2:8 (which is about salvation grace) and are concluding with the Shepherd Psalm. It is quite simple: Until you stand in awe at the miracle of your own salvation, the miracle of his gracious providence will fail to move you. His grace is not self-evident until he has given us new eyes with which to see and new minds with which to understand.

Share with your mate your recollection of that moment of life when *God* became more than just a word for you.

Pray, thanking the Father for being all you will ever need or want.

Week 11, Day 1
THE PROMISE FOR LOVERS
Read Luke 6:38

It makes sense to follow our discussions of grace with a series on giving. Grace is giving. But grace is what God does and we can't. Giving is what we can do. By giving, we come closest to being what we were supposed to be in the first place, before the gates of Eden clanged shut!

Giving can be impersonal or intensely and intimately personal. (We are going to talk about intimacy on the last day of this week; so hang on!) Giving can be done with words, hands, presents, or by check. There is an enormous variety to the spice of giving, but one thing remains constant: "Give and it shall be given unto you." This promise came straight from the lips of Jesus and may be trusted totally.

Why, then, are we concerned that it may or may not be true? Is it too materialistic? Is it not spiritual enough to fit our pale images of Jesus? Or is it our fear of being suckered again? It takes love to reverse our attitude about giving. When you love someone, you start learning to give. That's why I call these words from Jesus the promise for lovers. They are the ones who are in the best place to learn the truth about giving.

The person who forgets about the consequences of being a possible sucker and starts giving and giving and giving will find out that the gates and windows of heaven have already been opened to him. It will be a "good measure, pressed down, shaken together and running over that will be poured into your lap."

Take three slips of paper each. Make them into love coupons that your mate can redeem later. On each slip describe something you are willing to do that your mate will particularly enjoy. Exchange your love coupons.

Pray, thanking the Father for helping you to learn and know the joy of giving.

Week 11, Day 2
THE LAW OF THE HARVEST
Read 2 Corinthians 9:6-11

A stingy, successful farmer is a contradiction. He may be stingy with people, but he can't be stingy with the land. No one can plant sparingly and reap bountifully. Can you imagine a farmer planting only half of his rows and expecting a full harvest? As the Bible points out, the land teaches us unforgettable lessons.

The irony is that people who understand the land forget that there is only one law of the harvest and that it applies to people just as it does to the land. The Lord of the harvest meant for all of his creation to respond to the same principles. What is true for the land is true for us all. "Whoever sows sparingly will reap sparingly and whoever sows generously will reap generously."

The reason for the uniformity is found in the mind and purpose of the Father. It is his desire to give to the two of you all you need and more.

That is just about the best bargain you will ever find. There are, in fact, only two *ifs*. One is his purpose in providing this unlimited bounty. He will make you rich so that you can be generous on every occasion. God is not part of making anyone a private millionaire. If he makes you rich, it is so you may become a pipeline of giving.

The other *if* has to do with his method. If you give much, you will get much. If you give little, you will get little.

Does this sound like a radio evangelist trying to talk you out of your money? We are really talking about the secret of a successful marriage. When you learn to give to one another and to others, you are in the best position to receive God's blessings upon your home.

Talk together about what each of you can give your marriage in order for it to grow.

Pray, asking the Father to teach you how to be good farmers even if you never see a plow.

Week 11, Day 3
DON'T RUIN A GOOD THING
Read 2 Corinthians 9:5

Today's passage teaches one of the most profound lessons about living and loving. The apostle Paul had a burden on his heart about the suffering which the Christians were enduring in Jerusalem. Because hard times had come upon them, he wanted to make sure their needs were taken care of and that they knew how much he loved them. Some of the Jewish Christians thought Paul had no use for them. Others thought he was a heretic. He was not willing for their suspicions to keep him from loving them. Everywhere he went he asked for an offering for the church in Jerusalem.

Paul had presented the plight of the Jerusalem saints to the church in Corinth. Their response was open and generous. But Paul knew that the Corinthian Christians were immature and impulsive. They were good at making promises which they did not keep. And like most people who make promises and don't keep them, their spiritual growth and fellowship were being affected.

If we were to translate Paul's advice to an impulsive congregation into suggestions for a contemporary marriage, the result would be something like this: "Don't ruin a good thing by letting your promises and intentions drift along." The most sacrificial promise is only as good as the act which lives it out. Impulses and promises are whispers from God to help us become open and generous with one another. Don't turn the sweet into sour by letting your promises limp away unlived.

Each of you make a list of three promises which you are willing to make to one another. Indicate the date by which you will do these things. Share your lists. Then plan ways of doing each.

Pray, confessing to God that some of your best intentions have never been acted out, and asking for his help in keeping those promises you make to one another.

Week 11, Day 4
MAKING GOD SMILE
Read 2 Corinthians 9:7

Do you remember how you worked to get your parents to smile? It was something different at each age. As a preschooler you made them smile by being cute. As you grew older their smiles came as you increased in your understanding of responsibility. Competition, good grades, nice friends, graduation, a good job—these were the things which brought a smile. The big smile—plus a few tears—came on the day you got married to someone they really liked. Many things pleased them and made them smile. But there was no one thing which you could always do to make them smile.

The Father is different. One thing always makes him smile. "The Lord loves a cheerful giver." It is not just our gifts to God that makes him smile. He smiles when he sees us becoming what he made us to be. We are made in his image, and he is the eternal giver. He means for us to be givers, too. When he sees our gifts, small though they be, this pleases him.

Does all this sound a lot like salvation by works? A legalist and a cheerful giver are a million miles apart! Their reason for doing things tells the story. The legalist does what he has to do to keep from getting squashed. A cheerful giver does what he decides to do to meet the needs of others.

Recall together times when your mate surprised you with a gift. Share your remembered feelings of those times.

Pray, confessing to the Father that a lot of times you give only what you think you have to give, and asking him to help you feel free to give cheerfully from the heart.

Week 11, Day 5
OUTDOING EACH OTHER
Read 2 Corinthians 8:1-7

Benjamin Franklin was not an especially religious man. But he loved to hear the British evangelist George Whitefield. Whenever Whitefield preached in or near Philadelphia, Franklin was sure to be present. Because he knew that there would be an appeal for the orphanages which Whitefield founded and supported, Franklin always left his money at home. Invariably, though, when Whitefield made the appeal Franklin would borrow money from those around him to make an offering.

The apostle Paul also knew how to motivate people to give. While telling the Corinthians about the needs of the church in Jerusalem, he mentioned the response of the Macedonian churches. They had outdone themselves in their sacrificial giving. So Paul turned to the Corinthians. Just as they had excelled in everything they ought now to excel in one more thing—this offering. He threw down a challenge: Outdo each other.

Paul's reason for issuing this kind of challenge was not merely for the sake of those in Jerusalem. Paul knew the Corinthian church was hurting terribly because they were so self-centered. He called them out of their concern only with themselves. He urged them to outdo themselves in doing something for others.

All of us face the danger that we will become our own prisoners. The way out of that is to practice the generous art of outdoing ourselves for the sake of others.

Recall together recent times when your mate did a spontaneous, thoughtful thing. Affirm one another for that. Then talk about those things which squelch the spirit of generosity.

Pray, asking God to help you respond sacrificially to one another's need.

Week 11, Day 6
SWAPPING LOADS
Read Galatians 6:1-5

One of the recurring fears of childhood is not getting as much as other people. Another is the fear of having to do more than somebody else. I have experienced both fears. I've counted the presents under the Christmas tree. I've also cried out indignantly about the injustice of having to wash or dry the dishes more often than my sister. You may have similar memories.

Unfortunately, adults have fears of having to do more than others. That is why Paul had to write to remind Christians how they were supposed to behave.

The Galatian Christians were being seduced into legalism, and they were judging each other. So Paul told them that, if they desired to do the law, let it be Christ's law of love. The way to fulfill the law of Christ was and is to carry each other's load.

Such an instruction can awaken all kinds of fears of people taking advantage of you. People are just not dependable. If I don't watch out for me and my rights, no one else will!

There are three things to keep in mind if you start feeling that way. First, there are some things which no one may carry for you. Second, there are also some things which no one ought to carry alone. Third, when you swap these loads, something wonderfully redemptive happens to you in your relationship.

Take time to talk about these matters with your partner: What are your fears about having to do more than your share? What kinds of burdens can you legitimately share? What do you think will happen if you swap loads?

Pray, confessing to the Father your anger when you think others are not pulling their load, asking his forgiveness, and asking him to help the two of you swap loads.

Week 11, Day 7
TRUE CHRISTIAN SEX
Read 1 Corinthians 7:3-5

We finally got around to it. We promised to do so on the first day of this week. For eleven weeks now we've been talking about many other things; perhaps you've wondered if we would ever discuss sex. I am sure you have been enjoying this extra-special dimension in your relationship.

You may have been wondering, however, if the Bible talks about how Christian husbands and wives may express themselves sexually. You bet!

Christian couples are not merely permitted to have sex; they are encouraged to do so. This is a Christian responsibility. It is one of the vital ways in which we help to meet one another's needs.

Also, we may not assume that sexual activity is a magnanimous gesture on the part of one or the other partner. While neither partner may grasp, neither may withhold sexual relations from the other.

The reason is that in a Christian marriage husbands and wives no longer *own* their bodies. They now belong to one another. To withhold sexual relations is to deny this spiritual instruction. To give ourselves joyfully and fully to one another is to affirm that which God has already declared to be true.

No one should assume that we may fulfill this law of Christ if we simply *lend* our bodies to one another. The responsibility for entering fully into this mutual giving is vital.

There are times when sexual activity should cease; but this should only be temporary and by mutual consent. As soon as that reason is passed, we need to engage again in helping and affirming one another sexually. To be casual about this part of our commitment or to deny one another is to place ourselves under the strain of needless temptation. The bonding of sexual intimacy is essential to full faithfulness.

Take a moment and share your response to this teaching from the Bible. Share any fears you have about the intimate giving in sexual relations. Be open and caring about your mate's feelings.

Pray: "Father: Help me to give myself fully to my partner so that I may realize the joy you have in store for us."

Week 12, Day 1
QUID PRO QUO
Read Philippians 4:15

In our church we think children are important, and we schedule special activities to be sure they know that. For example, every other Sunday we have a children's message. This is mainly a time when I can be one of them again.

One year on the Sunday after Halloween I suggested that the kids might want to share their trick-or-treat candy. This struck a very sensitive nerve. It is one thing to put Daddy's nickels or quarters into the offering plate. It is an altogether different matter to give real capital (their candy). The next Sunday one young boy handed me a sack of candy he had collected. He had decorated the sack with flowers and with the phrase "It is more blessed to give than to receive."

It is more blessed to give than to receive; but have you ever thought what would happen to giving if there were no receiving? Receivers are as important as givers.

We all know persons who receive but never give. We don't have many good things to say about such people. We also know people who give but won't receive, and somehow we ascribe a kind of nobility to that type of person. Why? If a person refuses to receive because of pride or because it might obligate him to others, he may be giving because of pride or to obligate others. What is so noble about that?

Giving and receiving are Siamese twins. They are reciprocal. The person who truly gives is the one who continues to remain open to receive. *Quid pro quo* means something for something. That is the way the flow stays open in the tides of love.

Lovers are givers. Lovers are receivers, too. Sometimes the hardest thing for a lover to do is to be willing to be a receiver.

Take a few moments to share your responses to this question: Do you sometimes discount your mate by refusing to receive that gift which is given in love?

Pray, asking the Father to deliver you from the pride that keeps you from receiving fully and openly.

Week 12, Day 2
RECEIVING IS GIVING
Read Luke 23:42

Yesterday we started thinking about something which is foreign to our usual thoughts. We emphasized the importance of receiving in a loving relationship. Too many times we have interpreted love as being a matter of giving. The receiving part was an embarrassment which had to be endured; but the true love was in the giving. The truth is that many times the most loving thing is to be a gracious receiver.

Every parent knows what it means to a small child when his raggedy gifts are received with enthusiasm. Receiving is a way of giving.

Think about how today's verse applies to this truth. You may have wondered how this verse could have anything to do with receiving. I hope you were able to read all of the story (Luke 23:32-43). It is one of the most moving events which took place on that tragic hill. The feelings being expressed from all sides indicated to Jesus that the people involved did not need anything he had to offer. As the scene shifts to the crosses, one man picks up the jeers of the crowd. He doesn't need anything Jesus has, either. But the other man, also a criminal, saw how much he needed what only Jesus had to give. He asked Jesus to give him the imperishable gift. Jesus, who never turned anyone away when they asked, answered him with words of hope and promise.

To receive what Jesus has to give is to give him what he wants to receive: yourself. I have nothing to give him but myself; but in order to give him me, I must receive him. That is not only essential to salvation; it is vital to any true love relationship.

The person who says "I want to give you everything" is not really telling the truth, unless he also says "I need you and what you are and what you give." Receiving is also giving.

Share with one another at least one way in which you need to be received by your mate. Talk about ways you can work together to make your giving and receiving more open.

Pray, asking the Father to help you to be ready to share your needs openly with one another.

Week 12, Day 3
DON'T YOU TRUST ME?
Read John 13:6-8

Peter is center stage again. Aren't you glad the Bible features people who have clay feet? We've encountered Simon Peter before, and for the next few days, we are going to witness him trying to upstage Jesus.

Jesus was doing two things: First, he was preparing his disciples for his death, which was imminent. Second, he was giving them a model of servanthood which was to be the life-style of his people.

Every time Jesus talked about service, the disciples kept changing the subject to who would get the key to the executive washroom in the Kingdom. They simply could not or would not understand that the Kingdom was not made up of bosses but of servants.

There was no more menial task than washing road dust from travelers' feet. This was the job assigned to the low man on the totem pole. The picture of Jesus doing this job was too much for Peter. He was never above rebuking Jesus for what he considered to be behavior unfit for the Messiah.

When Jesus got to where Peter was seated, he refused to let Jesus minister to him. He refused to receive what Jesus wanted to give. Just like us, he had all kinds of *good* reasons why he could not let Jesus wash his feet. Of course, Peter wasn't thinking of himself; he had to rescue Jesus from this awful spot. Just like us, he found excellent ways to rationalize his refusal to fully participate in the flow of love. Jesus' response was, in effect, "Peter, don't you trust me?"

That is what love always says to reluctant receivers. When we refuse to let ourselves be on the receiving end of love for a change, we are demonstrating a lack of trust.

Share with one another a time when your mate refused to accept your gift. Discuss how you felt when your gift was rejected.

Pray, asking the Father to help you be willing to let your mate love you.

Week 12, Day 4
I DON'T NEED NOBODY
Read John 13:8

Watch any little child's frenetic activities and you can discern a straining for independence. "I did it by myself" is the prelude to "I don't need nobody." In its bluntest form this was what Peter was saying to Jesus.

The only person who could really say that he doesn't need anyone is a deaf, blind person who lives alone in a wilderness. Even then the wilderness is a gift from God. Helen Keller came close to being just such a person, cut off radically from the rest of the world by her deafness and blindness. But it was not until she quit saying "I don't need nobody" that she was able to begin receiving the loving help of Annie Sullivan.

We were made both to need each other and to fulfill ourselves and others in our interaction. We deny our creation and function to pretend we don't need anybody else. Love always needs somebody else. Love alone is not love at all. Imagining that we are self-sufficient is as ridiculous as imagining a hammer doing all the jobs of the rest of the tools in the chest. Ever try to use a hammer when you needed a screwdriver?

We cannot function alone. This is especially true in relationships. We need each other. We need to be needed by each other.

Lovers who confess their need for what the other can do—instead of always professing what they are going to do—are giving love its best chance to grow. It isn't easy to confess a need. There is always a chance of being turned down or rejected. But love needs, and love takes the risk in confessing that it needs.

Take time to confess your need for one another. Share your feelings about being needed.

Pray, asking the Father to deliver you from any notions of self-sufficiency.

Week 12, Day 5
I'LL NEVER TELL!
Read John 13:8

Love is tender. Love is tough. Not just tough in hanging on in trying circumstances, but tough in confronting situations which threaten love.

Simon Peter thought he was showing his love for Jesus when he refused to let Jesus wash his feet. Jesus, in love, had to confront Peter and help him understand that he was, in fact, threatening the very existence of the relationship. He told Peter, "Unless you are willing for me to do anything I want in your life, we can have no relationship at all." Sometimes love has to get tough in order to make love grow.

This is probably no great surprise to you. After all, you had some very clear understandings before you got married. You both clearly understood that dating around was over. It didn't have to be spelled out that it was a matter of great importance whether you were faithful or not. There were probably some other things about which you had a common vision.

There were also some things which you should have talked about, but you never did. Perhaps you assumed that love always knows how to act right. By now you know better. Some things have to be spelled out.

Love doesn't mean I'll never tell when something is bothering me or threatening our relationship. Love means that I will tell you because our relationship is worth it.

Jesus' confrontation with Simon Peter saved their relationship. If Jesus had sorrowfully moved on around the circle, Peter would still be wondering what had happened to the best friendship he'd ever had. Are there some things in your relationship which need some straight talk? That is not a confession that the whole thing is a failure; it is a realization that as imperfect as we are, we need regular checkups in the ways we try to love each other.

Share your feelings about how difficult it is to confront one another. Talk about how the two of you need to share tough love at times. Assure one another that confronting means you love your mate more, not less.

Pray, thanking the Father that he has given you someone who cares enough to confront in love.

Week 12, Day 6
I'M NOT GOOD ENOUGH
Read John 13:8

Why should people ever refuse attention? There seems to be no good reason for it, but many people consistently and systematically reject attention. But inside they crave it! If you compliment such a man's suit he will say that it was the only thing left in the closet. If you praise a special meal such a woman spent hours preparing, she will point out that the rolls were in the oven too long. Every attempt at a compliment or praise or expression of affection is met and pushed aside. This is known as discounting.

Discounting is reducing the value of something. We know why salespeople discount sales items, but why do individuals discount the attempts of others to praise them? Perhaps it is because they do not see themselves as worthy of such attention. Such humility may be noble in some areas, but it is destructive in relationships.

A person who discounts loving attention is not only expressing a certain feeling about himself (*I am not good enough for all this fuss*), but he is also discounting the person who is paying the compliment or expressing the affection (*you are not really telling me the truth about me*). What seems a charming, self-effacing custom initially always becomes a source of frustration later. How do you praise someone who refuses it?

I think part of Peter's problem was that he did not feel worthy of Jesus' attention. He discounted Jesus' attempt to minister to him: "I'm not good enough for you to wash my feet." He wasn't *good enough*, but that had nothing to do with what Jesus wanted. For Simon to find the blessing which he needed and wanted, it was necessary for him to quit thinking in terms of worthy and unworthy and simply receive that which was offered in love.

On separate sheets of paper, write for one another five compliments. Begin each with "I like the way you . . . . " Then read your lists to one another. Be careful to accept, not discount, the compliment of your mate.

Pray, asking God to help you to receive openly and thankfully the love you give one another.

Week 12, Day 7
RECEIVING IS LOVING
Read John 13:9

Say what you will about Simon Peter, he never overreacted to the point that he withdrew and shut up. When he saw his mistake he was ready to correct it immediately. When he saw the blunder he had made in not being willing to let Jesus wash his feet, he got it all straight in a minute. If washing feet is essential for the relationship, then don't stop there; wash everything!

Blundering is a part of the danger of being a human being. We never blunder so frequently or so grandly as when our relationships are involved. People whose success is assured in other fields of endeavor are often real disasters when it comes to friendships. Even lovers get cranky and step on each others' toes.

Blunder free is not the goal, though. It is the willingness to respond with a spontaneous openness which sees the mistake, takes proper action, and expresses a desire to do whatever is needed to get the relationship where it ought to be.

Openness and spontaneity are not automatic. We are by nature sinners, and sinners try to hide. To be open and spontaneous takes a desire translated into action. I want to be that way toward the one I love, and I decide I will be that way.

Perhaps the most delightful part of Peter's response to Jesus' clear confrontation was that, instead of arguing with Jesus, he immediately put the issue in perspective. Quickly he made himself ready to do things the way Jesus wanted. The important thing for him was his willingness to receive what Jesus wanted to give. Receiving is loving.

Have you found out some things about the way you are receiving the gifts of your partner? Have you learned of the joy of receiving fully the attention of your loved one? Don't stop now!

Take time to share what you have learned about yourselves this week. Have you found new ways of being open to each other? Talk about them.

Pray, thanking the Father for giving you someone who loves you enough to be patient with you.

Week 13, Day 1
CHOOSING YOUR SPIRITS
Read Ephesians 5:18

We have finally come to the most bothersome topic in marriage: submission. For some people this passage in the Bible is all trouble. For others it is the panacea to all trouble. The truth is that both are right. It seems impossible to choose to be submissive and carry it out in proper fashion. Even if outwardly you are in the posture of submission, inwardly you may be waiting for a chance to get things rightside up again! However, such submission would solve nearly all of the problems in relationships.

Is submission in marriage possible? The Bible says that it is all a matter of what controls you. A person who is filled with wine is being controlled by the wine. We know that wine doesn't make choices for us, but it affects us so that we do not make decisions according to our normal patterns. A person who is filled with the Holy Spirit is controlled by the Spirit. The difference between wine (spirits) and the Spirit is that, while the wine is not a living, personal being, the Spirit is exactly that. When we are filled with the Spirit, it is the Spirit who makes decisions for us.

That may sound like a cop-out; but, in fact, it is the way God enables us to do those things which lead to our true happiness. Being filled with the Spirit does not mean doing away with your own personality. You have to make the decision to be filled with the Holy Spirit. You must live out the decisions that are made under the control of the Spirit.

The Holy Spirit wants each of you to be like Jesus. The greatest joy in Jesus' life came as a result of his constant, willing submission of his will to the Father's will. What was true for Jesus in his earthly life is certainly true for us. Submission is the key to spiritual growth and marriage enrichment. Who or what controls you? That is the question.

Take a moment to share your feelings about the word *submission*. Does the idea of submitting yourself to another scare or threaten you?

Pray, asking the Father to help you understand what submitting to Christ means. "O Father, help us learn to risk ourselves with You. Fill us with your Holy Spirit."

Week 13, Day 2
THE TEST OF WORSHIP
Read Ephesians 5:21

Since people get so upset over the subject of submission, just how important is it?

Submission is essential to the proper expression of what it means to be "in Christ." The problem is that we have confused submission with the power games which people play.

The number 1 game among human beings, even among husbands and wives, is *King of the Hill.* As a child, you remember how much fun that was—for a while. For many, somehow, somewhere along the way, it ceased being a game and became a life-style. It is an inherently destructive life-style. People are destroyed and families are destroyed when such power struggles take place.

The only way submission works is for both husband and wife to decide mutually to follow the example of Christ. Both must love, forgive, give, receive, and so forth, the way Jesus did. In fact, look back over the last two weeks of devotional topics and you'll see a pretty good list of the elements which make up submission.

This is why submission is so vital. Submission is not a way in which we make people bend to our will. In fact, submission, as the Bible teaches it, is a voluntary way we respond to each other because of our primary relationship to Jesus Christ. "Submit to one another out of reverence for Christ."

Submission is a true expression of our worship of the Lord. If he is Lord, we delight in placing all parts of our lives under his direction. Submission is what he wants.

Talk together about ways you get yourselves into one-up or one-down positions with each other. Share with one another three ways you seek to meet the needs of your mate because of a teaching of the Bible. Then discuss how doing such things expresses submission.

Pray, asking God to work in your lives to bring about mutual submission to one another. "Father: help us to level with you—and with each other."

Week 13, Day 3
BODIES NEED HEADS
Read Ephesians 5:23

One reason some people find Paul's teaching on submission offensive is that it seems to put all the burden on wives and give husbands an excuse for being authoritarian and domineering. Aside from the fact that this does not represent Paul's teaching at all, it certainly would not solve the problem. Any husband who has been weak-minded enough to try to force his wife to do things *willingly* has found her to be anything but joyful and open. Joyfulness and openness are keys to whether true submission or mere knuckling under is taking place.

Paul's teaching about the husband being the head of the wife as Christ is the head of the church, his body, seems to add fuel to the fire of misunderstanding. How does this head and body concept add to our understanding of true submission? Some interpreters have insisted on an autocratic model based on Christ's absolute sovereignty over the church. It is unreasonable to suppose that God intends for any human being to have that kind of power over any other.

The interpretation which captures the idea best for me is that which takes seriously the vital relationship between a head and a body. They are bound together, each deeply affecting the other. It is only as they act responsibly and submissively toward each other that the head does not suffer from headaches and the body is free from stomach ulcers or heart murmurs.

Submission is always voluntary, or it is not biblical submission at all. Submission is always mutual, or it does not fit into the biblical ideal (Eph. 5:21). A home in which the Holy Spirit has led a husband and wife to find the vital head and body relationship is a gift of God's grace.

Review together your process for making decisions affecting both of you. Who decides? Which kinds of decisions require both partners, and how do you make the final decision in those cases?

Pray, thanking the Father for showing us in his relationship with Jesus what submission is.

Week 13, Day 4
JUST LIKE JESUS
Read Ephesians 5:25

I am always surprised when people accuse Paul of hating women or seeking to lock them into a second-class status. Obviously they have not read Paul carefully. If Paul called on anyone to carry the heaviest burden in the relationship of marriage, it is the husband.

In his discussion of mutual submission he calls on husbands to relate to their wives as Christ related to the church: "He loved her and gave himself up for her." If you have any doubts about what that means, turn to those portions of the Gospels dealing with the crucifixion or read Philippians 2:5-11.

Think of the implications. Could a husband try to force his wife to do his will if he were loving her as Christ loved the church? Could he be comfortable with bringing her pain by his casual neglect if he gave himself to her and for her as Christ did for the church?

Husbands who complain that their wives do not meet their needs probably have never submitted themselves to their wives as Christ submitted himself to the church in love and sacrifice. The man who tries to excuse himself by claiming that his wife is different is only ignoring his own unwillingness to love as Jesus does. I cannot imagine any person in any normal relationship who could be insensitive to that kind of love.

Let me ask you husbands a tough question: Are you sincerely attempting to love your wives as Jesus loved the church? Are you not only willing to die for her, but also to live for her? Does she know how extra special she is to you? Anything less is less than the Holy Spirit wants to make possible in your home.

Share with one another any times when someone tried to make you feel second class. Talk about how the love of Christ helps you to feel first class.

Pray, asking the Father to help you learn to love as he loves us.

Week 13, Day 5
WHAT'S A BODY FOR?
Read Ephesians 5:28-29

Perhaps because husbands are a little thick-headed sometimes and caught up in trying to be macho at other times, Paul has to tell them twice what it means to be submissive in their relationship with their wives. He uses the metaphor of the body. Men ought to treat their wives with the same common sense they use in the care of their own bodies. No one hates his body, but he feeds and cares for it.

How does a person treat another person as if she were his own body? Have you ever seen a man go through the discipline of exercise and diet in order to keep his body in shape? Or have you ever seen a mother bathe a tiny baby? What tenderness and care she shows as she washes and dries and powders that beloved little body!

A body is to protect and care for. A body is to enjoy. That is the element which I think slips out of most marriages. The reason why so many couples do not enjoy one another is because they fail to care for and protect one another. A body which is neglected as much as some wives are would not allow any enjoyment at all! It would be tired all the time, way too tired to do anything exciting!

This is one of the most practical instructions that Paul ever wrote. A lot of husbands might not understand what it means to love their wives with the sacrificial love of Jesus, but any husband can figure out what it means to treat his wife with the same care and consideration he shows his own body.

Enumerate with each other three ways you can cultivate a sense of importance to each other. Help each other express what would be good for you.

Pray: "Father: help us to keep investing our attentions so that our marriage will remain vital to us both."

Week 13, Day 6
THE PROMISE FOR CHRISTIAN HOMES
Read Matthew 18:20

So we come to the end of the journey. Not your journey, of course. But my journey with you is over. I thank you for letting me share in one of the best times of each day. I hope that these have been times of insight, learning, sharing, and prayer. I hope you have learned the value of a time together with the Lord. The patterns you set will determine the directions you take in your service for the Father. He rejoices in your love for one another. You remember that it was "for this reason that a man shall leave his father and mother and be united to his wife, and they will become one flesh."

I wish I could guarantee you that, if you did everything I suggested, yours would be a trouble-free marriage. I wish, but it isn't so. My advice isn't perfect. So even if you followed it to the letter, there would still be flaws. We have no control over our circumstances, and sometimes there are forces and situations which press down upon us so heavily we scarcely get by. There will be times when hard decisions must be made, and you will not have enough information. There will be great trials and temptations. For times like those you must remember today's passage: "Where two or three are gathered together in my name, there I am with them."

Perhaps you thought that verse was for people at prayer meeting or saints under persecution. The home was God's first institution. The church is merely the larger family on its way to the eternal home. This is a promise which is for Christian homes. You are gathered together in his name. Claim his promise: "I am with you." He is not merely the unseen guest; he is the Lord of your manor.

Join hands and let me pray for you: "Father, I thank you for the blessings you have given and will give to these, your children. Watch over them. Keep them close to you and close to one another. Help them to learn how to love. Give them the joy that comes only to those who have learned the lessons of the cross. Grant them your perfect peace. In Jesus' name, Amen."